Still Lickin' the Spoon

Other books written or cowritten by Becky Freeman

Worms in My Tea and Other Mixed Blessings
Adult Children of Fairly Functional Parents
Marriage 9-1-1

Still Lickin' the Spoon

the Spoon

And Other Confessions of a Grown-Up Kid

Becky Freeman

BROADMAN
& HOLMAN
PUBLISHERS

Nashville, Tennessee

4262-79
0-8054-6279-1

Published by Broadman & Holman Publishers, Nashville, Tennessee
Acquisitions and Development Editor: Vicki Crumpton
Page Design and Typography: TF Designs, Mt. Juliet, Tennessee

Dewey Decimal Classification: 248.84
Subject Heading: CHRISTIAN LIFE—HUMOR
Library of Congress Card Catalog Number: 96-53396

Library of Congress Cataloging-in-Publication Data
Freeman, Becky, 1959–
    Still lickin' the spoon (and other confessions of a grown-up kid) / Becky
Freeman
        p. cm.
    ISBN 0-8054-6279-1 (pb.)
    I. Title.
PN6162.F74   1996
813'.54—dc21

                                                                96-53396
                                                                CIP

97 98 99 00 01 1 2 3 4 5

For My Family of Origin
Daddy, for teaching me to listen to the rain.
Mother, for making everything all better.
My brother, David, for showing me how to chill and be real.
My sister, Rachel, for reaching out to all of us
with her child-heart.
The child I was, am, and ever hope to be
is grateful, indeed, to be growing in this family.
I love you all.

❧

Contents

Acknowledgments

B revity is not my strong suit when it comes to thanking the dozens of people who help create and produce a book. So many faces float in front of my mind, and each of them makes me smile for different reasons.

Thank you to my husband, Scott, for freeing me to write and grow, for good-naturedly taking the kids out for pizza as deadlines loomed close, and especially for loving me even when I'm more obnoxiously *childish* than charmingly *childlike*. You are, pure and simple, my hero.

Thank you, Zachary, Ezekiel, Rachel Praise, and Gabriel. You've not only been wonderful sports letting Mom tell your stories; you've risen to the level of shameless hams. Bless you, my children! Because I get to be your mom, I will always be rich.

Ruthie Arnold is not only an incredible mother but also my teacher. Thank you for passing on to me the gift of laughter and the love of words. And, Daddy, I always remember your praise, always your love. If you ever criticized me—even once—I cannot recall it. Thank you both, for giving me roots and the reassurance that my wings really would hold me up.

Hugs and thank-yous to Lori Smith, Marilyn Deuell, Mary Johnson, Melissa Gantt, Gracie Malone, Fran Sandin, Tina Jacobson, and, finally, Deborah Morris and the Round Table. Because you, my friends, regularly invite me to come outside and play, I do not go stark raving mad or climb the walls of isolation.

To Bob Briner, friend and mentor, for opening my eyes to the most effective ways to share God's love. Bless you for the encouragement you've brought to so many—from famous artists, athletes, and executives to a little-known gal from the boonies of East Texas. Because of your inspiration, hundreds are lighting candles rather than shouting at the darkness.

Thank you, Mike Hyatt, for being an advisor on this project and a friend in this life.

Finally, to my Broadman family. I do not say this lightly: Broadman & Holman is more than a publishing company. This is a family of fun and caring people who also happen to be top-notch at what they do for a living. Warm-hearted thanks to:

- Vicki Crumpton, my editor and friend. You are that rare combination in a person: one who is able to give on-target critique coupled with generous praise, both at the same time.
- Colyer Robison, for being the most cheerful and encouraging publicist on the planet. (Has anybody *ever* seen Colyer so much as frown?)
- Greg Webster, for being ever-serene in the midst of all life's storms—publishing and otherwise. You and your wife, Nancy, are "Young at Heart" personified—how blessed are your six children!
- Bucky Rosenbaum, for listening and for your prayer on a difficult day. (By the way, I couldn't write about Winnie the Pooh without thinking of you.)
- Trish Morrison, Rene Holt, Susan Linklater, and Becky Yates for taking me in from the cold on my first all-by-myself-out-of-state trips—and into your hearts and homes. You've gone far and above the call of PR duty and have crossed over, permanently I'm afraid, into the realm of Buddy-dom.

So many more names I'd love to mention from the B & H family. But it would take a whole chapter to thank each of you for your warmth (both in person and over the phone), your enthusiasm for our books, and for the behind-the-scenes work you put into helping these words ultimately reach someone's heart. Please know that you are much appreciated.

To the readers of my books. It is a high honor when anyone takes time out of a busy life to attend to someone else's thoughts. Thank you for letting me share with you. It is your input and feedback that continue to give me assurance that I am not alone in this lovely, loony thing called life.

And finally, to Abba, my Father. I cry with joy that I am Your child!

Can't I Just Grow Up to Be a Kid?

Eight-year-old Gabe hugged his side of the car as I swerved to avoid a tree and almost hit a mailbox in the process. Backing my station wagon out of the driveway is still not my forte.

Our original wagon, the Titanic, which some of you may remember from *Worms in My Tea*, eventually sank—much to our teenagers' delight. For three lovely months thereafter, I drove an almost-new, quite sporty Ford Explorer. Two small fender benders and a smashing encounter with a Winnebago, however, put me back in the driver's seat of our current nerd-mobile.

My husband, Scott, believes it is fate. Or God's wrath. Or a twisted joke. There he is, a red sport truck hunk, coupled with a station wagon woman. Even the car's "wood-grain" panels are in reality sun-faded contact paper. To add insult to Scott's injury, it also droops down in back, like a toddler's overloaded diaper. Our older children—Zach, Zeke, and Rachel—appropriately nicknamed this car, Sag. But, as Gabe will tell you, "It's real, whole name is Sag, the Tragic Wagon."

The one blessing of driving a station wagon is that there is plenty of metal around me and my kids—and folks can see me coming from afar in time to swerve out of my path.

"Mom?" Gabe asked, grabbing for the books flying off the seat as I rounded a corner on three and a half wheels.

"Uh, huh," I answered, absently pushing all the wrong buttons as I searched in vain for the radio knob. I knew I was only half listening to my child, but I simply can't listen to children *and* operate heavy machinery at the same time. Groping for the radio, I activated the cigarette lighter. *Well, that'll sure come in handy,* I thought, *if I take up smoking in the next ten minutes.* The next button I pressed turned on the windshield wipers. *Wrong again. Not a cloud in sight, and here I am driving down the highway with the wipers waving, "Alert: the driver of this car is clueless!"* The next knob sent a stream of water up the front of the windshield. *Well, maybe it's a good thing those wipers are in motion after all.* By this time, with my windshield and dashboard in full swing, I could not remember what it was I'd been searching for in the first place. So I flipped on the radio, hoping the music would eventually jar my memory.

That's when I heard Gabe's voice again, seeping into my consciousness.

"MOMMM!" he was now shouting as he waved a paper napkin back and forth in front of my face. Then, carefully enunciating his every word, as if I were hard of hearing or spoke a foreign language, he said, "Mom. Are-you-pay-ing *at-ten-tion?*"

"Yes, Gabe. You can lower the flag. What is it?"

"I was thinking."

"Uh-huh?"

"I was thinking how you are really smart in math and how you write really good books and stuff."

"Well, thank you, Sweetheart."

"But, Mom," he stopped there, a look of concern wrinkling his brow. He glanced up at the wipers, which were, at this point, methodically smearing hazy twin rainbows of grime across the windshield. Then, turning his eyes back to me, he finished his proclamation. "Did you *know* that you have *no sense at all?*"

There was no animosity in his statement, no trace of sarcasm. He'd just been observing a typical "Mom scenario" and out popped a logical conclusion, the cut-and-dried truth. He felt he should warn me—for my own safety, I suppose—that my mind, however seemingly intact, should not *ever* be counted on to provide a shred of common, useful sense.

Now I've known about this mental deficit for a long time. Many others have gently hinted as much throughout the years. But I'd never heard it stated with such blunt accuracy: "Sure, you are smart, Mom, but you have *no sense at all.*" Like the classic tale of the emperor and his new clothes, a child will openly declare what everyone else dances around.

Art Linkletter once said, "I can say, after a lifetime of interviewing, that the two best subjects are children under ten and folks over seventy. Both groups say exactly what's on their minds without regard for the consequences: the kids don't know what they are saying; the old people don't care!"[1] But, perhaps Oliver Wendell Holmes best summed it up when he wrote, "Pretty much all the honest truth-telling in the world is done by children." The lesson is this: If you ever really want the flat-out truth, visit an elementary school or a retirement villa. Ready or not, they'll let you have it.

A few days after Gabe's honest evaluation of my mental state, I was wracking my "senseless" brain trying to think up a title for this book. So I turned to our resident eight-year-old for advice. After all, Gabriel had been the source of inspiration for the title of my first book the day he gifted me with a writhing nightcrawler in my glass of iced tea. The title worked amazingly well, too, drawing attention to the cover until the stories inside had a chance to grab hearts. *Why mess with a good system?* I thought.

I found Gabriel lounging around on the living room floor, his feet propped up on the couch cushions above him. He says this position makes the blood heat up his head. Taking advantage of his warmed-up noggin, I asked him the million-dollar question.

"Hey, Gaber-Doodle (his nickname du jour), what do you think I should call my next book?"

Like a trained psychiatrist, he answered my question with another question.

"Well, what do you want the title to make people do?"

Honestly? I thought. I looked around at the furniture with its frayed upholstery and our one-bathroomed, in-process home for our family of six. Then I mentally calculated the balance of my checking account.

"To tell you the truth, Gabe, I want people to like this book so much that they'll buy lots and lots of copies. And I hope when they read the stories inside, they will smile and remember that sometimes it's good for grown-ups to act more like kids."

It took him all of two seconds to come up with an answer.

"OK, Mom, you should call it, *Buy This Book, It's Really Good.*"

I laughed. It was an isn't-that-cute sort of chuckle tossed out as I strolled by and patted my son on the head. But I couldn't get Gabe's title out of my mind. *Buy This Book, It's Really Good. Buy This Book, It's Really Good.* I had to admit it had a certain charm in its unbridled honesty. It also reflected my personal goal in writing this book: to see the world from a more honest, child-like perspective.

I knew I wanted the chapter titles to be phrases and questions kids might say. Why not the title too? Interestingly, childhood questions are often the questions I'm *still* asking as an adult. Inside childlike declarations and singsong sayings lies a surprising abundance of wisdom.

Gabe's idea held on as the working title for this book until the time came to set it in stone. That's when it dawned on us that *Buy This Book, It's Really Good,* though catchy, didn't really describe the book's contents. And secondly, I kept having nightmares of some disgruntled reviewer (with no literary taste, of course) changing the title to *Borrow This Book, It's So-So.* But now we were back to the drawing board.

One evening as I was scraping a bowl of chocolate icing and sampling a taste from the spoon, a feeling of nostalgia swept over me. For a fleeting moment, I could almost see myself as a child, barely tall enough to peek over the kitchen counter, hurrying to ask Mother if I could lick the spoon before my brother or sister beat me to it. *What's great about being a grown-up,* I thought, *is that I'm still lickin' the spoon—only I can do it whenever I want, without waiting my turn.* As it turns out, there was a title buried underneath that spoon full of chocolate, and it's decorating the book that you hold.

Aren't we all really kids anyway, dressed-up in disguise? As I quickly approach the Big 4-0, I'm more determined than ever to brighten up, loosen up, and live it up in whatever time I have left on this earth. Who better to observe than children to find out how it's done? Forget the *Seven Habits of Highly Effective People;* bring on the *Habits of Highly Effective Preschoolers!* A gathering of grown-ups was told long ago, by the wisest Teacher of all, that they were simply going to have to behave more like children. "For such," He declared, "is the kingdom of heaven" (Matt. 19:14).

I am a storyteller—more artist than teacher, painting parables better than expounding principles—so there will be no lists of lessons or numbered habits. Instead, as an artist draws a butterfly or a mouse or some such symbol into every painting, it is my intent to draw into every story an imprint of your own childhood remembered or a present bouncing-around-my-living-room child. Or perhaps, even more often, it will be a glimpse of the children we still are inside. And through the telling of simple stories, I hope lessons will subtly appear and fall where they may into hearts that are hungry for the touch of a child.

If you had a wonderful childhood, perhaps these stories might sprinkle some forgotten joy or trigger a poignant memory into your grown-up days. If your childhood was anything but wonderful (in retrospect, was anyone's perfect?), this book is written especially for you. As the saying goes, "It is *never* too late to have a happy childhood." Most of us have spent a lifetime growing up. How'd you like to join me for a bit of *growing down?*

A little child will lead them.

ISAIAH 11:6

&

Can I Hold the Baby
One More Time?

Tonight I participated in a scientific experiment. It's something I've not done in nine or ten years, though there was a time when I frequently gathered the necessary drugstore supplies and waited—with hands wringing or pressed together in prayer—for the bathroom/lab results.

Tonight I took a pregnancy test.

I took the test even though my husband, Scott, has had the big No More Babies Surgery (the granddaddy of *all* baby-stopping surgeries to hear him tell the tale). It also goes without saying that I haven't had a clandestine affair or anything. Besides the fact that I am committed to my husband, I signed a publishing contract stating that my services could be dismissed should I fall into "moral turpitude." (Sounds like paint thinner to me, but I think it's some sort of legal term meaning, "Please don't embarrass us unless, that is, you can write it up as family entertainment." I'm pretty sure that a clandestine affair would be considered a tad turpitudish.) Anyway, I was late, and when a woman is late she knows that sometimes, occasionally, the impossible happens.

In case you're holding your breath, the rabbit didn't die. The criss didn't cross. Nothing, and nobody, turned blue. I am still a "me," and not an "us." Looks as though Zach, Zeke, Rachel, and Gabe will be our "quiver complete"—with no surprise arrows being flung our way.

I didn't cry, of course, because the possibility of being called "Mommy" again had been ridiculous from the start. Imagine a woman in her late thirties with three teens and a third grader sitting up nights in a rocking chair cradling the well-diapered bottom of a newborn, patting a cloud-soft nightie draped over tiny shoulders, baby's breath gently tickling her neck . . .

OK, OK, I'll admit it. I've always been a sucker for babies. When I was about seven years old, a beautiful dark-haired woman at our church gave birth to a beautiful dark-haired baby girl. As soon as I spied the mother and baby in the church nursery, I began praying that someday, somehow, I'd get to sit next to them in a pew. "And please, God," I'd add, "let it be before the baby grows up and gets too big for a first grader like me to hold."

Then one glorious morning, it happened. The young mother sat down, holding the priceless bundle of mysterious sweetness, *right next to me.* I was beside myself, immediately plotting—as only a seven-year-old can—how I might take advantage of this once-in-a-lifetime opportunity.

If I can just scooch over close enough I might could, real real gently, touch that soft little baby's head. And if I can make my face look sort of sad and wishing, the lady might say to me, "Would you like to hold my baby, Becky? After all you're getting to be such a big girl! Why, I can tell just by looking at your face, you're going to make a real good mommy someday." Yep, that's what she'll probably say. If I look at her just right.

Unfortunately, as hard as I twisted my face with all angst and earnestness, the new mother didn't "read" my facial expressions. I'd have to *verbalize* my longings—a terrifying thought. I was so shy; I rarely spoke to grown-ups other than my parents unless they first spoke to me. However, when it comes to a chance at holding a real live baby, a little girl's gotta do what a little girl's gotta do. The last chorus of "Now the Day Is Over" droned to an end as I mentally rehearsed my speech and gathered up my courage. The congregation stirred to leave. The men jingled their keys; the women adjusted their gloves and pillbox hats. I cleared my throat, and it all spilled out in one breathless plea.

"Could I please hold your pretty baby girl for just one minute if I promise-cross-my-heart-hope-to-die I won't drop her?"

Thankfully, the mother must have seen the courage it took for a bashful child to blurt out such a heartfelt request. Before I knew it I was holding a real live baby right in the middle of church where everyone could see what a big girl I was. And I knew the entire congregation would be whispering, "Look at that Becky Arnold—what a good little mother she's going to make someday. Do you see how tender she is with that new baby?"

The real baby girl turned out to be much heavier than I'd imagined. Until that moment I'd only rocked two other babies—my stuffed Baby Thumbelina, and my stiff-jointed plastic doll that drank *and wet* orange Kool-Aid. After the minute had passed, my small arm began to quiver from the weight of the baby's soft-hard head. Still, I loved the warm, breathing, squirmy feel of this *live* baby doll. When the mother reached for her child, I relinquished my treasure with great reluctance. I had just been given a glimpse of "mommy heaven."

It was only surpassed, years later, by the intensity of holding *my own* real live babies. I didn't know I possessed such a fierce protectiveness until I heard my first child cry. Though I was weakened from a long labor, I would have wrestled a samurai to get to my newborn son and quiet his fears.

My beautiful babies . . . where did they all go? I look into the eyes of my children now—all of them stretching toward puberty or young adulthood—and search for signs of the helpless infants and chubby toddlers they once were. Here and there I catch an occasional glimpse—a lisped word, a mischievous glance, a gentle pat on my shoulder. Does every mother harbor a secret wish that she could bring back her newborns for just an hour or so?

Like Emily, from Thornton Wilder's play *Our Town,* I sometimes wonder, "Do any human beings ever realize life while they live it—every, every minute? Oh, what I think when I see my youngsters growing up, the precious moments of childhood racing by. How can I squeeze every last second of fun, excitement, and sweetness out of those strange little creatures who are ours for so short a time?" On a wall above my childrens' crib, I hung a cross-stitched poem, reminding me to squeeze the joy out of these fleeting years.

Dishes and dusting can wait till tomorrow
For babies grow up, we've learned to our sorrow
So quiet down cobwebs, and dust go to sleep
I'm rocking my baby and babies don't keep.
ANONYMOUS

Thanks to this poem's insistent message, the housework waited for most of ten years. (Perhaps that is why Scott periodically asked if he could replace it with the quote, "Cleanliness is next to godliness.") But I cuddled and rocked my babies until their feet dragged the floor.

Honestly, now that I've failed the pregnancy test, I'm relieved to be passing up all the pain that comes with an impending birth—swollen ankles, morning sickness, contractions, dirty diapers, confinement, car seats, potty training, runny noses, and every mother's favorite plague, impetigo. As I've stated from the beginning, it would be preposterous for me to cry—at this stage of the game—over not getting a positive mark on my test.

However, if the crisses had crossed, or the dot had turned blue, I'd have found some way to cope with all the childbearing "downers." Most likely, I'd have dreamed of a well-padded baby's bottom, cloud-soft nighties, and feathery breaths tickling my neck. Even at my age, I might have made a good little mother—just once more.

Oh pooh. Where's a tissue when you need one?

From the lips of children and infants you have
ordained praise.
PSALM 8:2
❧

This chapter is dedicated, with love,
to Rachel and Grace Webster.
Welcome to the world, little ones!

TWO

Do I Glow in the Dark?

S cott and I have finally done it. We've graduated from preschool. Well, actually, it is our *children* who have graduated from preschool. We, more accurately, have officially completed all required labs in Preschool Parenting. Funny, this new stage. As I've already admitted, there is a certain melancholy sadness in bidding farewell to the childbearing, toddler-chasing years. But have I mentioned the waves of euphoria that also come with this time of transition?

There is something akin to giddiness in knowing that never again will it be *my* candy-crazed toddler having the temper tantrum at the grocery checkout. Not only that, but Scott and I are now free to spoil other people's children with nary a thought to the consequences. We get to be like fairy godparents to our young nephews and neighborhood children—perpetual nice guys. There are three little preschoolers down the street whose standard greeting to us is, "Do you have a treat for me today?" Scott almost always has a stick of gum or a piece of candy ready for such occasions. If only real parenting were as easy as handing out goodies.

When our son, Zachary (now sixteen), was about eighteen months old, my Aunt Hazel came for a visit. Before long Zach started in with some well-timed whining and foot stomping around the vicinity of Aunt Hazel's knees. Her automatic response to his fit of passion was to kiss him on the forehead and place two gooey cookies in his dimpled hands. I started to give her that don't-spoil-him look, but before I could say anything Hazel slapped her hand on the counter and matter-of-factly said, "Becky, how would you like my advice on raising children?"

"Sure," I replied, eager for any help I could glean at this stage of the game.

"OK, here it is: Give them everything they want; don't ever say no."

I smiled as I raised my eyebrows. "Is this the method you used to raise your son?"

"Of course not. It's my advice on how you should raise my great-nephew."

Now that I'm an auntie myself, I'm free to adopt Aunt Hazel's childrearing advice—to be used only with other people's children, of course. Take, for example, my nephew, Tyler.

First of all, I should explain that Tyler glows. There is no other word to appropriately describe this child phenomenon. By "glowing" I mean when this kid smiles, he smiles all over. The grin that starts at the corners of his mouth spreads out like ripples of water to his dimpled cheeks, moving upward to his eyebrows, causing them to pop up and down with excitement, the lights dancing in his eyes below. Giggles flow freely, not only from his mouth, but seemingly from every joint in his body.

Tyler is also very small for his age. Though he is six years old, he has the tiny build of a child of about four—giving him an almost elf-like aura. I'm always picking my nephew up, without thinking, and loving on him as I would a toddler. When I first saw him last summer, I ran to hug him and then lifted him off the floor in a huge bear hug. He was polite. He even managed to give his crazy Aunt Becky an obligatory pat on the back. But I was startled when I heard his very grown-up voice over my shoulder insisting, "Aunt Becky, I'd like you to put me down now. I was about to go work on the computer."

This spring Tyler came to visit his Uncle Scott and Aunt Becky and all his country cousins at our lakeside home while his daddy, my brother David, went fishing in our area. His mother, Barbara, who is a wonderfully organized mother, had to stay home in Indiana. Before Tyler's visit, she called to brief me on his routine.

"Becky," she said, as always, distinctly enunciating her words, "Tyler usually goes to bed at 8:00 P.M., and it is very important that he do some school work while he is there so he won't get behind on his studies. I'll pack a fresh change of clothes and underwear for every day—you know how picky he is about staying clean. He knows how to brush and floss his own teeth, of course. And he really shouldn't have too much sugar or junk food because it tends to make him hyper."

Barb, please forgive me. I must confess that it only took one week under my watchful care for your son to go completely to pot. Somehow we never got around to the homework. I have no recollection of the toothbrush, though I think we did try using the floss for fishing line. And don't even ask me about the condition of his underwear. The only thing I'm sure that Tyler changed was his affinity for staying neat and clean. But we did manage to have some big-time fun.

For days on end, Tyler fished to his heart's content down at our lake pier (Tyler's "heart's content" averages about eight hours of casting and catching a day). When it comes to fishing, he is his daddy's own son. I remember when David was about Tyler's age, he dug a huge hole in our suburban backyard and filled it with water from the hydrant. There he sat, for hours, certain that at any minute he'd snag a whopper. (I'm sure our mother thought the hole in the backyard was well worth a few days of peace and quiet.) Our local paper even snapped a picture of David fishing at a nearby pond. He was holding three cane poles at once in his small clasped hands.

During most of Tyler's stay with us, he only set his pole down long enough to call up to the house for fresh rations of peanut butter and jelly sandwiches. Oh, and he'd yell for a jacket when the sun began to fade and the evening air took on a chill.

If Barb had seen her son at the end of a typical day at our home, I don't know if she'd ever let him come back. (She tells me she'd rather not know.) Basically, Tyler turned into a grimy ball of worm slime with fragrant splashes of perch and crappie lingering about his hands. However, Tyler could never get dirty or smelly enough to cover his glow. And so, when he flashed his big grin and asked me to take him to the store for fresh minnows, I rarely, if ever, said no.

On the way home from such a trip to Gantt's minnow/deli/ convenience store, I happened to glance in my rearview mirror toward the back of the station wagon. There sat Tyler, all aglow, a chicken leg in one hand and a lollipop in the other. He was contentedly alternating fists with bites and licks. It was awfully cute, but I was soon lecturing myself.

Now Becky, you are spoiling this child just because he's your nephew and he happens to be adorable. You've got to quit being such a gullible old softy. What will you tell Barb? That he ate balanced meals because he always had food of equal weight in both hands?

Late one evening, shortly thereafter, I realized things were totally out of control. Wandering into the kitchen I found Tyler perched on a stool behind the counter. He was obviously a kid on a mission. He'd taken two half-gallons of Blue Bell ice cream out of the freezer and positioned one on either side of himself. (If you don't know about Blue Bell, just ask any transplanted Texans in your area and watch their eyes glaze over.) The lids were off both cartons, and Tyler held a spoon in each hand, poised for action. I started to protest, but then he looked up at me with a grin that glowed as big as a Fourth of July sky.

"Man, I love this place!" he declared. "I've had ice cream for supper two nights in a row now."

OK, I know it's awful. But I can't help it. I just can't find it in my heart to say no to a child who's about to glow. Besides, it was only one week out of a year; how much harm can one little week of nonstop sugar and worm dirt do to a kid?

This fall, David and Barb allowed Tyler to come for one more visit. As they were making preparations for this second trip out, Barb called ahead. She was as nice as she could be, but I could tell she was still struggling to recover from Tyler's last visit with us.

"Hi, Becky," she said, "just wanted to go over Tyler's routine. Again." (How can I blame her? She must have been thinking, *Let's try this once more—with* feeling.)

"Oh, Barb," I apologized, "I'm sorry we got Tyler so off schedule last time. You know how crazy things get around here. By the way, did you get the package I mailed after he left?"

"Yes," she answered with measured calmness, "and I really do appreciate you mailing Tyler's homework back. I understand you finally found his workbook in the back of your station wagon under the minnow bucket. Actually, that's sort of what I was calling about. Since we are taking Tyler out of school for the week, do you think you could encourage him to actually *write* something on the worksheets this time? Fill in some blanks, underline a sentence, circle something? I don't care if he stays clean. I can even handle digging the worm dirt out of his pockets when he gets back home. And a week without flossing won't cause his teeth to rot out. But if he can just do some homework this time—all I ask is *the homework*."

As I tried to give Barb my most reassuring response, I heard Tyler in the background yell, "Tell Aunt Becky to be ready to whip out the Blue Bell when I get there!"

What can I say? I rushed right out for a carton of Vanilla Bean and one of Cookies and Cream.

When Tyler arrived at our house this time, he felt easily at home, settling into a routine right away. (In other words, he didn't open his suitcase for the first two days.) One afternoon, when it was raining too hard to fish, Tyler sat and watched a Power Robo Something cartoon on TV. In response to the action on the television, he abruptly yelled out, "Awesome!"

"What's awesome?" I quizzed from the kitchen.

"Nothing," came the serious voice, followed by a heavy sigh from the living room, "I'm sorry, you're too old to understand."

Well, perhaps he is right. (I believe Oscar Wilde once said, "I am not young enough to know everything.") But this much I do understand: Tyler most definitely has the upper hand in our relationship. Even his insults seem cute to me these days.

Toward evening that same day, my glowing but exhausted nephew crawled up in my arms and fell asleep on my lap. When David walked in the door to take his son back home, I looked down at Tyler's sleeping form and then back up at David. On reflex, a little-girl question tumbled out of my mouth: "Can I keep him?" David chuckled, strolled over to stroke his son's hair, looked at me gently, and shook his head no. It was a painful good-bye.

But good news! I am going to see Tyler again soon. This time we'll meet in Virginia where the whole clan is gathering at my sister's for Christmas. I'll have her adorable four-year-old, Trevor, to spoil too. I only have one problem. How am I going to transport two half-gallons of Blue Bell ice cream on the airplane?

What am I thinking? If I'm considering going to these lengths to spoil my nephews, can you imagine me as a *grandma* someday? I wonder if there is a continuing ed course called, "How to Say No to Children Who Glow."

As I was pondering Tyler's glowing charm and my tendency to give in to anything he wants, I came across an intriguing quote by Winston Churchill. Churchill was one of history's *ultimate* charmers, and I believe I might have some insight into his ability to wrap the free world around his chubby little finger. One day he seriously intoned, "We are all worms." And then with childlike confidence and a gleam in his eye he added, "But I do believe that I am a glowworm."

In life, especially as we grow older, we are faced with two choices. Either we can let ourselves go, or we can find ways to glow. Why not go for the glow? I've noticed that people are more patient with the weaknesses of those who grin and giggle and enjoy life to the hilt. Whether this fact of life is fair or not, admittedly, could be argued. But take it from Tyler and Winston: The truth of the matter is, "people who glow rarely get told no." And when it comes to getting vital needs met—like finagling second helpings of Cookies and Cream—one must resort to any means available.

Those who are wise will shine.
DANIEL 12:3
&

THREE

'Cause It's Fun

E arly one morning this fall, Zeke—our fourteen-year-old—
slunk in from the back door and gingerly made his way
toward the kitchen. He was dripping wet and fully clothed. I
raised my eyebrows in a silent question as Zeke shook his head
and began to chuckle softly to himself. He weakly gathered up
the hem of his soggy shirt and wrung some water into the
kitchen sink in a futile effort to halt the puddling around him.
Then he turned around and looked me full in the face, as if to
be sure of my undivided attention. "Mom," he sighed, "you're
not gonna believe what Gabe's done this time."

Gabe is the quintessential "unique" little brother. He is and
has always been his own person—what some might even call an
odd duck. And speaking of ducks, it was literally an unusual-
looking duck that started Zeke on this morning adventure, leaving him drenched, shall we say, with fresh "Gabe news" to
report.

"Mom, I was sitting out on the dock this morning when I
noticed something funny-looking out on the lake. It looked like
a wounded duck caught in a trotline. So I jumped in and swam

toward the bird to see if there was anything I could do to help the poor thing. When I swam out for a closer look, my 'wounded duck' turned out to be nothing but an old piece of Styrofoam with a pencil stuck in it. And on the pencil there was a flag with a message in little-kid handwriting: 'Hi. This is Gabe. I just made this for the fun of it.'"

Just for the fun of it. Now there's classic "kid reasoning" for you. How often do we grown-ups do something off-the-wall or spontaneous just for the sheer, unvarnished fun of it? Probably not often enough. Kids, however, are masters at this.

I ran into a friend of mine, Angie, a couple of years ago. She'd just finished reading *Worms in My Tea* and was bursting with a story to tell me about her young son, Carson, who sounds as though he could be Gabriel's clone.

She said that one afternoon Carson found an earthworm on the back porch and began begging her to come see it right away. But Angie was busy vacuuming, so she explained to Carson that she'd come out in a little while.

"Becky," Angie reported, her eyes wide, "you will not believe what I saw when I finally came out to the porch. Carson had been *slinging* that worm around and around like a lariat rope over his head the entire time I'd been vacuuming."

"Oh, no!"

"Oh, yes! And did you know that earthworms *stretch?* I swear that worm was between a foot and eighteen inches long by the time I got to it."

"What did Carson say when you asked him why he did it?"

"He told me, 'Mom, I just thought it would be fun to sling a worm.'"

See what I mean? Grown-ups don't think like this. We see some worms, and what do we do with them? The bravest of us might dig them up and use them for fishing bait. But kids, like Gabe and Carson, are so much more creative. They think, *Why not let a worm take a swim in a glass of tea? Or better yet, try slinging one?*

The year I taught first grade was a perpetual eye-opener for me in terms of understanding kids' theories on fun—from stuffing wads of Play-Doh in their ears, to karate-chopping pencils into tiny pieces, to cutting designer shapes into their clothing. I'll never forget the afternoon, right in the middle of teaching a lesson, when one little boy abruptly dove out of his desk and landed on the floor at my feet. Later, as we sat in the office together, he innocently explained to the principal, "I sort of thought it would be fun to see how far I could jump out of my seat."

On another occasion, a shy little student walked up to my desk, opened her mouth wide, and silently pointed to a button she'd stuck to the roof of her mouth. Neither I nor the school nurse could dislodge it—the suction between her soft palate and the metal button was *that* strong. Her mother ended up transporting her child to the doctor's office to have it removed! The next day, when I asked the girl why she'd stuck the thing up there in the first place, her answer was predictable. "I don't know, Mrs. Fweeman, I just thought it would be fun."

As much as I do admire children's penchants for having fun, I realize, as an adult, I must temper my impulses. After all, I don't want to be sitting in a doctor's office with a button stuck on the roof of my mouth or forced to explain a wad of Play-Doh lodged in my ear. Though I've often fantasized about it, I cannot dive out of my seat and onto the floor every time I'm bored with a speaker's presentation. Sometimes I think the adult pendulum swings too far to the "let's behave" side, and we completely forget what it's like to have good, wholesome fun for fun's sake.

In an effort to bring more fun into my life I recently purchased a book called *Ten Fun Things to Do before You Die.*[2] It was written—believe it or not—by a Catholic nun, Karol A. Jackowski. This sister seems like a pretty fun nun (why do I keep envisioning Whoopi Goldberg?), the sort I'd love to meet for coffee and conversation. After forty-two years of living, Sister Jackowski declares she's found four ways to "have more fun than anyone else."

The first piece of advice she gives is to find fun people. Apparently, this is not an easy trick. Sister Karol writes, "One of the hardest things to find in life is fun people. Far too few appear and seemingly fewer survive adulthood." Suggested things to watch for on a search for fun people are: "good storytelling, perfect timing, interesting work, a good appetite, unusual sense of humor, fresh insight, and a brave daring life."

Advice nugget number two is, "Forget about yourself around other people. Not to do so is . . . just plain rude." I like this one; it's a good reminder for a self-centered person such as myself. Mother and I laughed the other day about how we sometimes feel burdened to *entertain* other people whenever we are in group situations—as if it is our obligation to provide the floor show or something. Not necessary, Karol says. "A good general rule is to think about yourself when you're by yourself, and in the presence of others, think and ask about them."

Third, she writes, "Be a Fun Person." To do this you must first make yourself interesting, and then be on the watch for opportunities that have the potential for great fun. Opportunities like "Clyde Peeling's Reptile Farm off the Pennsylvania Turnpike, any Dairy Queen, and, yes, boring meetings."

There *are* limits to fun, but not many. The fourth piece of advice from the Fun Nun is, "If it looks like fun and doesn't break the Ten Commandments, do it." Sounds like a good rule of thumb to me.

On a recent country getaway with a group of women from my church, I found myself gravitating toward one woman in particular. Right from the start Terry exhibited all the signs of being a fun person. In the course of conversation, we discovered Terry had traveled down the Amazon, been lost in South America, and had barely escaped a guerrilla's spray of machine gunfire. She'd also been a full-fledged hippie—her barefoot wedding taking place in a field of flowers. And though Terry has grown into a respectable Bible study leader, she's not finished being daring and interesting. Before the night was out, she handed each of us a drinking straw and with great gusto announced, "I am going to teach you all a new skill—one you can use to totally amaze and impress your kids, or even strangers in a restaurant."

Then, with all the dignity she could muster, Terry placed one end of the straw in her mouth and secured the other end, very carefully, into her armpit. Then she blew. For a few seconds we all sat motionless—stunned at the disgusting noises arising from the crevice in Terry's arm, and grateful we were not in a public place. But within seconds, we all began scrambling like crazy for our own straws to try the trick ourselves. Before I indulged, however, I mentally went over the Ten Commandments. When I could not find a deeply spiritual reason to abstain, I went ahead and blew for all I was worth. I only wish my teenage sons could have seen me in such top form. They would have been so proud. For reasons I cannot begin to explain, it was one of the most spontaneous, fun evenings I've ever had with a group of women.

Besides having fun with straws, we grown-ups could probably take a clue from fun-loving children and simply go outside and play more often. Like the poem said—"Dishes and dusting can wait till tomorrow"—they will still be their dirty old selves tomorrow, waiting for you to tackle them when you are in a better frame of mind. (I know, I've stretched that poem for all it's worth. Now that the babies are grown-up, I'm desperate for a new guilt-cleansing rhyme.)

I love the story from the Gospels where Jesus told Martha, Mary's compulsive-cleaning sister, to "chill out, leave the dishes alone, and come sit a spell with Me." (This is, by the way, my own very loose translation.) Why? He wanted Martha to get in on the conversation while she had a chance. After all, it wasn't every day that Jesus would be stopping by. The dishes could wait. Special opportunities, however, may not. How about this for an updated rhyme? "If you always wait 'til chores are done, you'll never, ever have any fun."

One sunny spring afternoon I had planned to stay home and be a good wife, maybe even cook a Sunday dinner, do the laundry, and read the paper. But then I had not just one, but *two* girlfriends call and ask me to go out to play. What could I do? I told Scott it was obviously the will of God that I go.

So I ended up in Dallas, soaking up sun on a quilt with my two friends. We were each eating a smoked ear of corn on the cob that was dripping with butter and covered with sour cream and bacon bits (to die for). Between stuffing ourselves and gabbing, we also watched magnificent, brightly colored hot-air balloons take off, one after another. With corn between my teeth and sour cream around my mouth, I grinned at my friends and slowly drawled, "I don't know about you guys, but I think this beats bleaching socks."

That Sunday afternoon, my family ended up eating sandwiches and cleaning up after themselves. What they didn't finish, I completed the next day. But what my husband and children *did* get out of the deal was a wife and mother who came home smiling and refreshed and happy to be alive. They agreed it was a pretty good trade-off.

So I say, sail that Styrofoam boat! Get that dusty kite out of the closet and fly it on a warm spring day. Ride a hot-air balloon, eat greasy fair food, blow silly noises through straws! Just do something each day on which you can look back and say, "I did that for the sheer, simple, childlike fun of it."

Eric Liddell, the Olympic runner from the movie *Chariots of Fire,* said some wonderful life-affirming words when questioned by his sister about his spiritual priorities. "Jenny, God . . . made me fast. And when I run, I feel His pleasure." Is it possible that we, too, might better "feel His pleasure" as we seize the moments God gives us full of pure, *unadult*-erated fun?

God . . . richly provides us with everything
for our enjoyment.
1 TIMOTHY 6:17

Let's Play Dress-Up!

I 've always believed in allowing people—including little people—the freedom to dress in ways that express their own personalities. Perhaps this explains why, a few years back, one visiting youngster asked me if he could "wear his shirt inside out and backwards like Zach and Zeke always do."

I, myself, have always worn originals. (At least people have always told me, "Becky, that outfit looks very *original.*") This has not been easy for my husband to accept, because he cares about blending in with society's norms when it comes to public attire. As one might guess by now, blending in with the crowd has never been top priority with me.

When Scott and I were newlyweds, all of eighteen and nineteen years old, my husband insisted we always walk, rather than drive, to our classes at the college campus located about a mile from our home. On chilly winter mornings, dressing for warmth, rather than for success, was my goal. My priorities made Scott more than a little nervous.

As I roved through the house, tossing layer after layer of whatever laundry was handy upon my shivering form, Scott would beg, "Becky . . . wait . . . *please* not the wool socks on your hands!"

"We've been through this a hundred times," I'd reply, digging through his sock drawer. "My hands get numb when they're cold and only your wool socks keep them warm enough."

"OK. Put footwear on your hands if you must, but that red bandanna you've been tying around the outside of your coat hood—*that* has to go."

"Scott, I need to keep my hood tied in close to my ears or the wind gets in there and makes them pound and hurt."

"Parading down the street with my bride dressed like a walking garage sale makes my *heart* pound and hurt."

"Ever since I was a little girl, I've dressed in layers to keep warm. My parents always thought it was cute—sort of a waif-ragamuffin effect. Anyway, I refuse to freeze my dirastecrutus for the sake of fashion."

"Just tell me one thing. When do you suppose you will be growing out of this rags and muffin phase? Listen, Becky, we all have to wave our good-byes to Puff the Magic Dragon, put away our pirate costumes, and move on from Hona-Lee." He stopped his lecture for a second, then scratched his head. "And what, pray tell, is a *dirastecrutus?*"

"I have no idea. But my mother always warned us never to let it freeze," I raised one eyebrow in warning, "and who knows what evil might befall you if it does?"

And so the conversation would end. Usually, we'd compromise. I'd wear the socks and bandanna, and Scott would walk a block in front of me, pretending not to know who I was. Little did I know that years later I'd get a small taste of what Scott had been feeling when my lastborn child insisted on dressing himself and parading the results in public. Unfortunately, I did not have the option of forcing my three-year-old to walk a block in front of me, pretending not to be his mother.

My youngest child, as you also may have already guessed, is—well, *different.* As soon as Gabriel was old enough to have a say in the matter, he refused to wear jeans and shirts like the other kids. Wearing them inside out and backwards wasn't even an appealing option to him.

It started out innocently enough. First, he began wearing the standard Superman cape. Just a portable plastic cape adorned with an iron-on *S.* No big deal except for the fact that he wore it every waking—and sleeping—moment. And it didn't take long for Gabe to move on to greater things. Batman came next, and his Batman cape of choice turned out to be my black half-slip secured around his neck by a large, pink diaper pin. (Wouldn't psychologists have a heyday analyzing that?) Eventually, the sight of my personal lingerie on display stopped bothering me, though it continued to cause Gabe's older siblings great fits of public humiliation.

It is important to remember these costumes were worn constantly, everywhere that Gabe went, twenty-four hours a day, for weeks at a time. To ask Gabe to go out the door without his costume would be like someone asking that you or me take a downtown stroll in nothing but our socks and underwear. Gabe's costumes *were* his identity: preschool power clothes. Without them—oh horrors—someone might mistake Gabe for a mild-mannered, average Clark Kent-type preschooler and not recognize him for the incredible, zowie-wow superhero he knew himself to be.

In October, things really began to get out of hand. Even I, who've always been proud of the fact that I'm a free spirit when it comes to matters of dress—not to mention immune to most forms of embarrassment—began to grow self-conscious when I left the house with my son. This, too, began innocently enough.

Several weeks before Gabe's fourth birthday, he commenced begging for a real fireman's costume.

"And Momma," Gabe insisted, "I don't want one of those sissy Halloween fireman suits. I want *real* fireman rubber boots and a *real* fireman coat and a *real* red fireman's hat. And 'specially I want a gas mask."

Silly me. I obliged. Oh boy, did I oblige. It was a cinch to find a tall pair of rubber boots. After much slicker-searching, I happened upon a bright yellow one—heavy-duty rubber with a hood. I even found a large plastic hatchet in a discount bin. The perfect red hat was ripe for the picking at a local toy store; it made a piercing siren noise when its button was pressed. (Within two hours, the siren's batteries mysteriously disappeared. Who in the world could have done that?)

But the coup de grâce—a sheer stroke of creative genius—was the "gas mask," which was actually one of those bright orange pollen masks that allergy sufferers wear when they mow the lawn. (My husband, by the way, is an allergy sufferer. But being the fashion-conscious guy that he is, he would rather be buried alive in grass clippings and found unconscious from a sneezing attack than chance being seen in public wearing one of these "nerd" masks.)

As you might imagine, the costume was a smashing success. For weeks that turned into months, Gabe wore the entire fireman ensemble—complete with gas mask—everywhere we went. Rain or shine. Cool weather or unseasonable heat wave. Gabe took his fireman duties seriously and stood ready to douse a fire or rescue someone from a burning building at the slightest sound of a smoke alarm. (Since our smoke alarm doubles as our dinner bell, he had quite a bit of practice.) I even have a much-prized picture of Gabriel at the mall, sitting on Santa's knee, dressed in his full fire-fighting regalia. Poor Santa had trouble understanding what my son wanted for Christmas, however, since Gabe refused to talk to the jolly ol' saint without his mask secured firmly over his mouth.

I don't remember what Santa actually gave Gabe for Christmas that year, but I do recall that my friend, Mary, gave Gabriel his best-loved present of the season. It was a long, polyester trench coat and a matching hat in a brilliant shade of yellow. From that day until Easter, Gabriel was Dick Tracy. I was so grateful to see my son's mouth ungraced by orange plastic and disposable filters, I welcomed Detective Tracy with open arms.

Today Gabe's growing up—and he has, surprisingly, adopted his daddy's taste in clothing preferences. Very aware of what's "cool," he now chooses clothes that help him blend with style into the world of third grade. The Superman cape, the fireman suit, and the yellow trench coat have all gone the way of imaginary dragons and other "fancy stuff."

"And what about Gabe's mother?" you ask. "Did she ever leave her childish ways behind and acquire some fashion sense?"

Well, it's like this. I'm about to go out for a walk. It's a cold and rainy day, so I'll need my hooded coat—and, of course, a pair of wool socks for my hands and a red bandanna to secure the hood so my ears won't pound and hurt. My husband? These days, he's proud to take long, meandering walks with me—no matter what I'm wearing.

All he asks is that I give him a good forty-five-second lead before I begin my walk—preferably, a good twenty paces behind him.

Your beauty should not come
from outward . . . clothes.
Instead it should be that of your inner self.
1 PETER 3:3–4

I'm Sorry, Frog

D riving in the car last night, one of Gabe's little buddies, Dallas, was relating a scene from the recent *Little Rascals* movie.

"See, the Little Rascals had this 'He-Man Womun Hater's Club.' And the kid with the real deep voice, the one they call Froggie, was telling his friends about a girl that had played a mean trick on him. But he got back at her. He took out a lizard and showed it to the *girl!*" Dallas exclaimed.

"So?"

"So, it scared her."

"Why?"

"Because girls are scared of lizards."

"Why?"

"Because they just are."

"That's not true. I know lots of girls who like lizards. If somebody showed me a lizard, I'd reach out and pet it. I'd love it!"

After all these years, it is still incomprehensible to Gabriel that any sane person could dislike a reptile or an amphibian. Like the title of Arnold Lobel's famous children's book states, *Frog and Toad Are Friends.* And according to Gabriel, they are *our* friends.

Though much of Gabe's amphibian/reptile-loving history has already been well-documented, the stories continue to abound. I began writing the material for *Worms* when Gabe was about three years old. He's nine now, and still as critter-loving a kid as I've ever seen. On his desk I recently counted two turtles, one frog, two hermit crabs, and—oh yes—about a dozen tadpoles swimming in—what else?—my best crystal bowl. I put up with a lot when it comes to matters of the heart. And for Gabe, frogs and turtles and tadpoles and such are definitely affairs of the heart.

Once, just once, in an effort to be "cool," Gabe broke his own little frog-loving heart. And I'll never forget it.

That fateful afternoon, Gabe burst into the house and dived onto my bed, wrapping a sheet tightly around his head. Being the sensitive and observant mother that I am, I sensed right away something might be amiss.

"Gabriel," I coaxed, "what's the matter, Honey?"

Nothing. No response from under the covers.

"Gabe, you can tell me *anything*. Have you done something wrong?"

There was a slight movement in the affirmative from the mummified form.

"Well, there's nothing you've done that can't be forgiven. Come on out and let's talk."

When he finally unraveled himself from the sheets I was taken aback by the flood of tears on his face and the obvious agony of soul in his eyes.

"What, Honey, *what?*" I asked softly, shaking my head and searching his face for clues.

After a few gulps he finally managed to say, "I . . . gigged . . . a . . . frog."

"Oh, dear," I said, remembering that Gabe's big brothers had been into gigging bullfrogs for sport, and then cooking their game's legs for meat. I'd never approved of it, but I know boys will be boys, and I tried not to think about the "frog hunting" going on in nearby ponds. And now it was clear: Gabe, trying to be a big hunter like his brothers, had taken a fork and "gigged" a small frog—thinking he'd bring home frog-leg "game" like the big guys.

"Oh, Gabriel," I said, "did it surprise you when you realized you had hurt something you've always loved?"

"Mo-o-mmm," he sobbed into my shoulder, his small fingers squeezing tightly into my arms, "I didn't think about it hurting him until it was over!"

I found myself swallowing lumps in my own throat all the while I was trying to convince my son he could be forgiven for his mistake. In truth, I wasn't stifling tears for Gabe's "heinous crime." It was because I identified with him so much. Have we not all, at one time or another, hurt something we loved and held dear? Haven't I "gigged" the ones I love the most with my careless or hateful words? And then suffered the weight of my guilt, wishing—oh wishing so hard—that I could turn back the clock and erase something awful I'd said or done? Every child, every man, and every woman has at one time or another come face to face with the fact that they've just gigged an innocent frog—that is, if they are still tenderhearted enough to admit it.

What to do, what to do? Dry the tears. Have a proper burial. And go back to loving frogs—this time with a deeper awareness of how precious and dear and inescapably beautiful are all the things that have been created by God's hand.

A few months after Gabe's frog-gigging crisis, he and I were walking hand in hand along our country road. Out from the woods, a box turtle lumbered into view. Gabe looked up at me and grinned toward heaven.

"Oh, wow, Mom!" he exclaimed. "That's two turtles in one day! Man, God's being good to me."

Gabe knew, as only a child can know, that all had been forgiven. And he also knew, instinctively, that God loved nothing more than showing off His frogs and turtles and toads to him. For it is our children—tender of heart and low to the earth—who are, most assuredly, the connoisseurs of creation.

*Be gentle and ready to forgive; never hold
grudges. Remember, the Lord forgave you.*
COLOSSIANS 3:13, TLB

Am I Cute?

G abriel has a friend living in the neighborhood now, which is a pretty big deal in this lonesome neck of the woods. Her name is Sarah, and she is eight years old. Now if someone asked me to choose a little girl who could epitomize my own "child within," Sarah would most definitely be in the running. Though she's a blue-eyed, cherub-faced blond—and I'm an olive-skinned brunette—I've decided we still have a lot in common. Our best hope of survival in this world is our ability to be really cute once we get ourselves into hot water.

Since Sarah's overactive conscience sometimes makes her honest to a fault, it is vital that she maintains her charm as she begins her truth telling. Otherwise, one might be tempted to wring her neck.

One April afternoon, the phone rang at my house and I heard Sarah's cheerful voice on the other end of the line.

"Happy birthday, Becky," she said.

"Oh, Sarah, how nice of you to remember!" I responded with genuine feeling.

"Well, I *didn't* remember." As I said, from Miss Sarah, one can always expect the unvarnished truth. I thought I'd help ease her conscience.

"It's OK, Sarah. You didn't remember yesterday, on my *actual* birthday, but you remembered *today* and it was so nice of you to call."

"Well, I didn't remember today or yesterday. Gabe just told me about it."

I was determined to be gracious about these belated birthday greetings, but Sarah was not making it easy.

"OK, Sarah, but you see, the fact is you called to wish me a happy birthday all on your own and that was a very nice thing to do. Thank you."

A loud silence followed. The angst on the end of the line was palpable, for Sarah is always compelled to tell the whole truth and nothing but the truth.

"Well, actually . . ." Sarah started. *Did I really want to hear what was coming next?* There would be no stopping Sarah until she had completely unburdened herself.

"Well, actually, Gabe *made* me call."

It was important that I get this straight. This child *was* telephoning me with a heartfelt and sincere-sounding birthday greeting. However, I was now to understand that Gabriel, my young son, was *forcing* her to do so. Silently I thought, *I get the picture, Sarah. No more explanations, please.* Anxious to put an end to this conversation before more true confessions poured across the line, I signed off in a hurry.

"Sarah, thanks for calling. You have made my day."

"Oh, you're welcome," came the sweet reply.

Not only are Sarah's "live" phone calls entertaining; the ones she leaves on my answering machine are equally popular. They bear perpetual testimony to her confused state of mind, with which I identify so heartily. When someone says, "Sarah left another message!" we all come running. For one thing, it took little Sarah a couple of tries to figure out that my voice on the other end was actually a tape recording and not me in person.

Her first recorded phone message went something like this:

"Can Gabe come over? What are you saying to me? Momma! Come here! Becky just picked up the phone and started talking to me, and I don't understand anything she said. *What?* Oh. *Is this a recording?* Oh. Well, I just don't know what to say. I guess I'm just pretty mixed up."

Ah, a girl after my own befuddled heart. If you know how to play your cards right, even confusion can be charming.

There was another message I almost couldn't bring myself to erase—it was left this summer while Gabe was supposed to have been over at Sarah's house playing. I later learned he had run home to go to the bathroom, but he'd neglected to tell Sarah he was leaving. When I checked the phone recorder later, Sarah's very serious message was blinking.

"Becky. I'm sorry to tell you this, but I lost Gabe. I can't find him anywhere. I'm sorry. He was here and now he is gone and I've looked everywhere. I don't know what else to do. We just lost him, that's all. I'm sorry, but he's gone. That's all I can say. I am really, really sorry."

Once again, I can relate to Sarah's message. If there is one underlying theme running through my own psyche, it is this: I am sorry. I am sorry I'm late. I'm sorry dinner isn't on the table right now. Or in the oven. Or even in little unprepared segments in the refrigerator. I'm sorry the house is a mess, and I'm sorry I've gained five more pounds. However, I am a Sorry Survivor. Let me rephrase that. I am a Survivor of Sorry.

How? I work really, really hard at being cute enough to compensate. Sometimes it does the trick; sometimes it backfires. But if you happen to be a child like Sarah, or an adult like me—if you find yourself being too honest for your own good, or in a constant state of confusion, or if you have a hard time keeping up with important things (like eight-year-old boys)—you may want to take careful notes. I recently pulled off a "coup de cute," and it probably saved my skin.

It all started after the Winnebago incident—the one that killed my once-spiffy Ford Explorer. Anyway, as I was rummaging through my purse after the accident, I came upon a tissue-thin piece of paper I'd forgotten all about. It happened to be a traffic ticket I'd received while driving on one of Gabe's field trips a few weeks earlier. (I had run a stop sign at the park.) Upon examining the fine print, I realized with some shock that I had missed the court date by ten days. Since Scott had recently bent another woman's fender, and I now had a major accident claim on my insurance, a thought occurred to me: *Maybe this is not the best time to have an outstanding warrant for my arrest.*

When I confessed my error to my husband, his expression didn't change—the way Clint Eastwood's doesn't change—and he retired to our bedroom to meditate. When he came out, his speech was prepared.

"Becky, listen. This problem could be disastrous. With another ticket, the insurance company could drop us and put us into a pool."

"Do you think they'll just throw us in with our clothes on and everything?"

"Becky, this is serious—you *know* what I mean. With Zach about to turn sixteen, our insurance will soar through the roof. I don't know how you're gonna do it, Honey. I know you're still shaken up from almost being splattered by a Winnebago, but you've *got* to charm your way out of this one. Godspeed."

The first thing that came to mind as I was receiving my marching orders was a bright orange billboard I'd recently seen on the highway. It read, "Traffic Tickets? No problem. Call 1-800-We-Fix-'Em." Or something like that. So my next move was to call a lawyer from the yellow pages whose advertising square looked most like the billboard. The deep male voice on the other end sounded fairly upbeat and hopeful as I described my case, until I told him the name of the judge on the bottom of my ticket.

"Ma'am," he quickly advised, "that's the toughest judge in the county. He doesn't cut anybody any slack once they've missed their court date. Just send 'em the money, and pray your insurance company has mercy on you."

I hung up, swallowed hard, and gave myself a pep talk. *OK, OK. So this judge is no soft touch. And sure, lots of women have tried and failed to cry or sweet talk their way out of a ticket in his court. But I must not give up. Scott's counting on me; he believes I can do this, and I have to give it my best shot.*

Just then my eyes fell upon a couple of my books and then to a chapter I had recently completed on the subject of my forgetfulness. It was called, "I Never Promised You a Rose Garden. Or Did I? I Can't Seem to Remember."

That's it! I thought, *I'll try to entertain him!* For the thirty minutes it took me to drive to the county courthouse, I conversed—nonstop and fervently—with the Almighty.

"God, grant me favor in the eyes of this judge and please, if You see fit, let him be a wanna-be writer." Human nature being what it is, I knew if the judge "had always wanted to write a book," he might very well be putty in my hands.

Upon arrival, I was ushered into the judge's chambers by a secretary in sensible shoes, who gave me little in the way of a greeting other than a pitying shake of her head. Sitting down on the edge of a cold vinyl chair in front of an expansive bench, I found myself opposite the Judge of No Mercy. Nervously, I cleared my throat.

"Your Honor, sir. First of all, I'd like to explain my situation—"

"Well, you can't," he said without looking up.

"Why not?" I asked, caught more than a little off guard.

"Because first you have to enter a plea. What will it be?"

"Insanity."

With that, he glanced up, and I thought I saw a glimmer of a smile. Perhaps I *had* found a soft spot after all. I settled on a more feasible plea of "no load contender"—or whatever it is—I told the judge I wanted the one that means "I'm not saying I did, but I'm not saying I didn't." This time he definitely smiled. Things were looking up, so I plunged ahead with my plan. I plopped two of my books, and the Forgetful Chapter, on top of the mahogany desk between us. His Honor's thick eyebrows stood at attention.

Thankfully, I had dabbled quite a bit in law, having read two John Grisham novels and viewed *The Firm* on video. And who didn't see more than their fair share of the O.J. trial? Patting the pile, and doing my best Marsha Clark imitation, I simply said, "Evidence."

Any balanced jury could have seen I was now on an unstoppable roll.

"You see, Your Honor, I'm sure lots of people come in and out of your office every day and *say* they forgot about their traffic tickets. But I have brought you undeniable *proof.* I actually make a living writing about all the things I've forgotten. Short and long-term memory loss is a handicap, as much as any other physical disability. But you can see from the evidence before you that I've determined to turn my disability into income and inspiration. So when I tell you that I forgot about the ticket in my wallet, you can believe, beyond any reasonable doubt, that I am telling you the truth."

He was quiet for a few seconds. Slowly, he eased his substantial body back in his black leather chair, scratched his chin, and sized me up with a raised brow. I gulped. What had I done now? Whatever it was, it was too late to back out. After what seemed like eons, he broke the silence.

"So you're a writer?"

"Yes, I am. I do so solemnly swear. I mean, I don't swear in my writing. I mean I swear I am a writer. Yes, Your Honor, I do . . . I mean, I am."

"You know, I've always dreamed of writing a book someday."

Oh, God, You are merciful to me! From that moment the judge and I were pals, friends—yes, even buds, if you will. He recounted tale after tale of life in a small-town courtroom. Why, before long we were laughing and slapping the bench and having a rousing good time. Then there was a knock at the door. The judge wound down a good story about a little old lady who'd told some amazing whoppers trying to squirm out of a delinquent ticket. Then good naturedly, he called out, "Come on in!"

The gentleman behind the door peeked in, his face a curious study.

"Thought I ought to check in on you, Judge. Sounds like you're having an awfully good time in here."

"Well, come on in," the judge said amiably. "Got a little gal here I want you to meet. She's real forgetful, so I've been trying to impress upon her the importance of putting outstanding traffic tickets at the top of her priority list. I'd sure hate to see her locked up in your jail."

With that, the judge smiled in my direction and said, "Mrs. Freeman, meet our chief of police."

Turning his attention back to the police chief, the judge spoke with mock sternness, "Listen, this young lady will need a police escort to the city limits. She's real accident-prone." Both men broke into a camaraderie of chuckles at my expense, but I couldn't have been more thrilled.

As I stood to shake the jovial judge's hand and take my leave, he informed me I could still take Defensive Driving to cover my ticket. I floated out of his office on wings of gratitude, but when I told the secretary outside that the judge had granted me mercy, she refused to take my word for it. She wasted no time picking up the phone and dialing his chambers. A few seconds later, the bewildered woman was staring at the receiver and then at me and back again at the receiver.

"Well, if that don't beat all. What in the world did you say to him?"

I shrugged and replied, "I just told him the facts, ma'am. Just the facts."

Not long after the incident, my mother sent me a greeting card in the mail. A note was attached to the front saying, "You might want to use this the next time you get in a fix with a judge." The front of the card shows a black-and-white photo of an adorable little girl, about five years old, wearing a rainslicker and a hat. She's holding an envelope in her outstretched hand.

Her facial expression is angelic, yet pitiful. Inside, the card reads, "Will you forgive me if I remind you how cute I am?"

Sarah, I have a feeling you and I will need all the "cute" we can get in this life.

Though there will be times when others may say we are maddening, I hope no one will say we are not entertaining. If we're very good, they might even say we have *charm.*

But just to be on the safe side, I think I'll tape the date for my defensive driving course to the dashboard of my vehicle. Now if only I can remember where I put the tape.

> *Standing in the court, she obtained favor*
> *in his sight.*
>
> ESTHER 5:2, NASB

ह

Would You Rub My Back?

I t was another one of those over-my-head, insufferably long church services. I was probably four or five years old. I laid my head on my mother's lap and curled my patent leather shoes up under the flounce of my dress. I remember Mother's lap being extra firm because she was wearing her full-strength Sunday morning girdle. My eyelids grew heavy as she absently stroked my hair and played with one of my curls. I felt loved, cuddled—her baby again. Then came—ahhhh, heaven in a church pew—my mother's fingernails, gently etching circles and curlicues and figure eights as they floated up and down my back. Even Big Church preaching could be tolerated under the influence of those hypnotic maternal hands.

Touch—the soothing power of touch.

When I was thirteen, I contracted hepatitis while on a youth trip—the form of hepatitis you get from drinking bad water in Mexico. Back home, in the wee hours of the morning, I couldn't eat, my side ached, I was weak. I had missed six weeks of school, and now my skin was afire with a rash—a side-effect of the jaundice. No amount of medicine, baths, or tears would halt the burning itch as it spread from my head to my toes. My mother, in the early morning darkness, sensed my misery—with good old-fashioned mother radar, I suppose—and padded down the hall to my bedroom. Once here she helped ease me from my bed to a comfortable pallet on the living room couch. Then, having done all a mother could do, she began to pray. Her hands rested upon my back, her words pouring quietly into the darkness.

"Father, I come asking relief for my Becky. Please grant her a good night's sleep." After that, all I remember is sliding into sleep with Mother's fingernails gently etching curlicues and circles and figure eights onto my back. The insidious itching, miraculously, was gone.

Touch—oh, the healing power of touch.

Fifteen. Sick again from bad drinking water on a summer mission trip to a foreign country. But this time I was still *in* the foreign country: Guatemala. I was riding on a rickety bus, with Scott sitting next to me holding me upright as his arm encircled my shoulders. I was not so sick, however, that I couldn't appreciate the delicious feel of Scott's skin next to mine. We'd not been allowed to show any physical affection during the summer until now, when the leaders relaxed the rules somewhat for our journey home. I will never forget the precise moment Scott reached over and took my hand; it felt amazingly tiny threaded between his strong fingers. It was wondrous, this hand-holding business, and I recall wishing there was some way we could stay linked this way forever. Then Scott said something that we both remember vividly, even after twenty-three years.

"Becky," he said with a boyish grin, as he stroked the top of my hand, "I have a feeling the sense of touch will always be an important part of our relationship." Now I know what you are probably thinking: There's a sharp line to use on a sick, vulnerable teenage girl. Think what you like; I happen to know my young heartthrob had the most honorable of intentions.

Wait a minute. Hold on. My husband is informing me that maybe it was just a wee bit of a line. But it worked. And he was right. Touch has been a special form of conversing between us for more than twenty years, connecting us in times of confusion, heartache, anger, passion, and tenderness—when words are either too clumsy or inadequate for the task.

Touch—the communicating power of touch.

We read about it in psychology and medical studies everywhere—this powerful, God-given force called human touch. Babies thrive on it and shrivel up and die without it. A simple hug has been shown to lower blood pressure and to release feel-happy endorphins. Even stroking a pet is healthy, they say, because there's something about touching a living, breathing *anything.*

A couple of years ago, Mother and I were interviewed at a local radio station. The host asked Mom for her best advice on raising kids. "Well," she said, "you pray a lot. You laugh often. And you keep touching them. When they're small, rub their backs, stroke their hair. As they become teenagers a quick neck rub or hand on their shoulder may be all they will accept. But don't stop giving your children some measure of physical affection."

No mother is perfect, but in this area, mine scores especially high. She's been given lots of opportunity to practice—not only with her babies, teenagers, and grandchildren, but also with the elderly. As each of our grandparents took their turn being sick and, finally, dying, Mother rubbed their tired feet with warm lotion; caressed their weary, wrinkled faces; held their love-starved hands.

Touch—the compassionate power of touch.

Even unto death. Perhaps, in fact, it is especially during occasions of grief and death that we find our greatest comfort in the voiceless compassion of a caring touch.

It was last summer. I was sitting across from my friend, Ruth, sharing a casual lunch of hamburgers, spicy fries, and soft drinks. The setting was average, everyday—just two women enjoying a lunch out. Anyone looking at us would have no way of knowing that one of us had passed through the death of her one-year-old son a few days before—a parent's ultimate nightmare. Yet even in the midst of her grief, Ruth managed to smile and occasionally to laugh.

Baby Caleb had been terminally ill since he'd drawn his first breath, so the element of shock was not as strong a factor in Ruth's grief as it might have been otherwise. But grief still comes. Her nursery stood emptied of its precious smiling, reaching content. Even so, Ruth, a young woman of boundless courage and determined joy, presses on, looking for the "good" in "all things." Her faith through this season of trial leaves me stunned with admiration. Still I know she aches, and I want so much to be of comfort. What can a sister offer another whose world has just fallen apart at life's fragile seams?

"Ruth," I asked tentatively, "can you tell me, other than our prayers, what practical things help at a time like this?"

She smiled as she retraced the events of the last few days. "Becky, even though Lee and I knew the end was always one breath away for Caleb, his passing still came as a surprise. I was in a fog all that morning of his death. Friends came with food, the youth group dropped by to clean house, mow the yard, and generally offer their services. All of that helped tremendously. But I still felt so uptight—so *anxious*. Then a couple of my closest friends sat me down and said, 'Ruth, we want you to think for a second. What do *you* need?' Then out of the blue, I found myself saying, 'I think I need a massage.'"

I laughed. "Had you ever had a massage before?"

"No," she answered, "I don't know why or how I knew what I needed. But God must have known. My friends arranged an appointment that very afternoon with a massage therapist named Adreena. And Becky, it was the strangest thing. It turned out to be exactly what I needed. I laid down on the table and Adreena began kneading away at the stress and sadness in my weary body. It was *wooonderful*. After months of nonstop caring for a critically sick baby, stroking him, attending to his needs, now I was on the receiving end of care. By the time Adreena finished with me, an hour later, I found I had the strength to get up and complete the funeral arrangements. My fuzzy head was more clear, and I knew I was going to make it through the day."

Touch—the life-affirming power of touch.

Ruth's testimony piqued my curiosity. I'd never had a massage. The whole concept of a stranger pouring oil on someone's body and rubbing them down seemed a little weird to me. Yet in many, if not most, cultures this practice isn't given a second thought.

As a matter of fact, I'd just read a passage from Suzanne Lipsett's journal, *Surviving a Writer's Life*. As a young student, Suzanne had been raped and assaulted. Since that time, she stayed emotionally numb. Seeking escape from painful memories, she traveled overseas and ended up in Istanbul. A series of circumstances landed her in the company of an aged, wrinkled Turkish woman. Much to her surprise, the old woman insisted on giving Suzanne a massage. The mothering, caring touch from this foreign woman sparked a turning point in Suzanne's journey toward healing. She wrote, "There was little left in me but gratitude to the woman whose hands had taken time to stroke and knead me. I was clean and warm, a child in the hands of an old, knowing woman whose very body spoke survival of her own nameless ordeals."[3]

Massage has been used for centuries to keep skin and muscles healthy and to relieve the stress of weary minds. My own youngest child begs me nightly for a back rub because it helps him fall asleep more peacefully. There must be something to it. But still . . .

Ruth assured me that Adreena was a trained professional—like a medical doctor. "Massage is therapeutic," many of my friends kept telling me, unflinching in their insistence that I must try it. I worried about disrobing in front of a stranger, even with a towel covering me. I possess several lumps and bulges—not to mention road maps of stretch marks—I prefer to keep under wraps. But then Ruth told me that Adreena was blind, and my excuses ran out. I made an appointment for a Tuesday afternoon.

Adreena turned out to be a pretty African American woman in her early sixties. She wore a simple cotton dress with her hair pulled up in a bun. When I walked into the room, she greeted me in a lilting voice. "Well, hello! I'm over here, Hon, be with you in a second."

I undressed and lay down on the table, covered only by a towel, and growing more uneasy about this idea as the seconds ticked by. I told myself this was just an experiment; I would be like a reporter on assignment. Adreena walked into the room, turned the radio to an easy-listening station, poured lotion on her hands, and started in on my neck.

Whoa. I was putty. I was a lump of dough. *Yes,* I thought, *I believe I can probably handle this assignment after all.*

While Adreena kneaded my muscles, I started a conversation. I began by telling her how much she had meant to my friend Ruth on a painful, heart-wrenching day.

"Ruth?" Adreena asked enthusiastically. "Oh, Honey, I liked her right away. She told me she'd just lost her baby boy. What can you say to a mother at a time like that? I just tried to love and comfort her through my hands. I believe my abilities are a gift and every day I pray that God will use me to minister love."

"Adreena," I mumbled as my body unwound in places I never even knew were wound, "what made you decide to do this for a living?"

"Well," she began, turning around to gather more lotion, "I like people. One good thing about being blind is that I honestly never think about a person's color. Their looks don't matter to me at all; it's their personalities and voices I remember. Also, I knew I'd be good at this because I do sincerely care about people. I've had massages, and I can tell the ones that are given with a sense of caring and the ones that are given out of duty. Without sight, all your other senses grow stronger. So I can tell a lot about people from something as simple as touch."

I closed my eyes and listened as Adreena went on to tell me how, as a little girl, she lost her sight after a series of operations for a brain tumor. She told of a mother who had wanted the best for her and, even though life was hard, had found a way to send Adreena to one of the best schools for the blind in the country.

As I lay on that table, I was getting a double whammy—refreshment for body *and* soul. Adreena's inspiration was infectious as she continued talking and kneading.

"You gotta have faith—in God and in yourself. Set realistic goals. When we do something we're a little afraid of—but we believe in ourselves and have faith and get it done—it strengthens us. My mother and my teacher and friends at the blind school all taught me these things and I'm here to tell you, they work. They made me believe in myself—and I've never been afraid to venture out."

While Adreena massaged my shoulders, arms, and hands, I discovered more about her life. She had once been married and now had two grown daughters. She spoke with her grown children almost daily, she said, but she's quite content to live alone. She talked of the exciting occasion when as a teenager she'd taken her first plane trip—a trip to get her first seeing-eye dog, a collie-shepherd named Susan. When Susan died after fourteen years of faithful companionship, it had been like losing a member of the family. Her children were heartbroken as well. Adreena never replaced Susan. She said she just never saw the need to.

"Do you ever get depressed, Adreena?" I asked lazily, curious to know if this lively woman ever suffered moments of despair.

"Now, I'm not Super Woman or anything," she answered as she continued working away with her magic fingers. "Sometimes I get down in the dumps and then I have me a good cry. Then I say, 'Lord I don't want to feel this way.' I hate those times. It's like an artery is plugged up in my spirit and I can't give out all the love and joy I want to be giving. Every Sunday morning, it's my job to give an inspirational statement at my church. Oh, they seem to love it, but I love it even more. I've got so much inspiration coming my way now, with people handing me quotes and verses and such, that I had to ask them to let me give two a Sunday."

Adreena rubbed my feet with a circular motion, and applied long firm strokes to the backs of my ankles. I melted. I vowed to teach Scott how to do this.

"Adreena?"

"Yes."

"Why don't you go ahead and give me the full treatment. Inspire me with one of your favorite sayings."

"Well, all right. Here's one of my favorites." She slowed down for effect, "With God's arms under us and His love around us we can face anything before us."

"Oooh, that's good." I turned over like a chicken on a spit to get the other side done.

"How's 'bout this one?" Adreena paused from her work a moment, adopting her Sunday morning voice. "Earth's worst often turns out to be heaven's best."

"Your church must be awfully proud to have you there," I commented. "Adreena, can I ask you one more question?"

"Sure."

"If you had to choose between being blind or deaf, which would you choose?"

I was unprepared for Adreena's depth of enthusiasm on the subject. "I believe I would have to choose to be blind, because there are much too many things I love to hear. I *love* music. Oh, how I love music! And the birds! How could I stand it if I couldn't hear the birds? I hear them sing, and I'm so thankful for their cheerful voices in the morning. And the sound of a baby's coo, and the little noise my dog made when she'd hand me her paw or lay her head on my lap! And the voices of my children. No, I can't even *imagine* not being able to hear!"

The thought of her children and grandchildren led Adreena to one last piece of advice before she ended my "therapy" session.

"And about children. Hon, you have to *listen* to children. They want to tell you things you may not think are very impor-tant, but you really listen to them—because it's important to them—oh my, how children need that. I used to read books, from Braille, to my children. They *loved* that attention. And when they were babies I nursed them because I knew the close-ness was good for them. Now my daughters want to do the same with their babies."

"Adreena," I observed, "because of your blindness I'm sure your children had more physical contact with you than most children have with their mothers, out of pure necessity. Maybe that's one of the many reasons you've had such great relation-ships with them."

She nodded and smiled as I rolled off the table, limp as a rag. I felt refreshed, renewed. I thanked Adreena for using her gifts—her warm, caring, mothering hands and her warm, caring, moth-ering words—to bless my day. I promised myself as I readied to leave, *I will definitely do this again.*

❧❧❧

That evening, at home, I noticed Gabriel tucked in his bed as I passed by his room. I paused to give him his favorite go-off-to-sleep back rub.

I also took the time to trace a few curlicues, circles, and figure eights on his back with my fingernails, which he liked very much. I told him he could thank his Granny. He looked up at me curiously.

Adreena told me she's flying up North to visit her grandchild this Christmas. I imagine her holding him close, reading to him from a book as her fingers fly across the colored pictures and dots of Braille. Just as she'd done with her daughters.

Touch—the cross-generational *blessing* of touch.

Paul went in to see him and, after prayer,
placed his hands on him and healed him.

ACTS 28:8

❧

I'm Gonna Marry a Hero!

Do you remember the first hero that made your little knees go weak? (Or, perhaps, inspired you to run through the house with your mother's lingerie secured around your neck with a large, pink safety pin?)

I was six when I found myself lovestruck over a cartoon rendition of Hercules. He was, I thought, the most handsome and well-drawn figure of a man I'd ever seen. I'd dream of being rescued from my kindergarten-small-potato life and swept away in the arms of my cartoon hunk. Even more interesting, I believed it could happen at any moment.

Then one day an awful thought crossed my mind. No, it wasn't that the man of my dreams was a comic-book drawing on a black-and-white screen. I never considered there could be any complications in carrying on a relationship with a cartoon. My concern went much, much deeper.

If Hercules flies out of the television set tonight to carry me off to Happily Ever-after Land, I can't even go! I don't have a single princess dress to wear!

So, in early fall, I began plotting how I might acquire a suitable gown should my Hercules come calling. At first, I tried getting a dress the surefire old-fashioned way: I whined. When whining failed to get the hoped-for results, I turned to my last resort: Santa Claus. On Christmas Eve, I don't think I slept at all. I was worried Santa might not be trusted to pick out a suitable princess gown. No matter how jolly and well-suited he was, Santa was still a *male,* and how could a man know what a little girl needed in a fairy princess dress?

Maybe Mrs. Claus helped him out, I don't know. All I know is that under the tree lay a perfect dress: silky blue and princessy pouffy with flounces of netting under the skirt. I nearly burst with gratitude. Thus, appropriately costumed, I spent many a happy hour imagining myself being carried away—all bedecked in princess blue—in the strong arms of my Grecian hero.

But then one day, as I was turning the channels (by hand—things were tough, kids, in the olden days before remote control), I found someone new. And suddenly, I realized my cartoon hero from Mount Olympus was much too one-dimensional. What I needed was a real man. A swinger. A man with minimal clothing needs. A man who knew how to hold meaningful conversations, even if they were with a chimpanzee.

During my Tarzan the Ape Man phase, I spent my summer afternoons imagining I was swinging from tree branch to tree branch with my hero of the month. I could perform a lovely female version of the famous "A-a-e-e-e-ah!!!" yell, accompanied by dramatic chest beating. I was sure if Tarzan ever swung by my backyard and overheard my mating call and saw how gracefully I could hang by my knees from the cross bar on my swing set, he'd drop Jane faster than a slick banana.

After Tarzan came Superman, then Prince Charming, and then the cute guy from "Lost in Space" took my fancy. Oh, I also took quite a shine to Robin. (Batman was too old for my taste.) From frontier survivalists to caped heroes leaping tall buildings in a single bound; from the adventurous to the supernaturally charming—I've always been a pushover for a hero.

Why this longing for a knight in shining armor? Feminists warn that these little-girl fantasies are harmful, leading us into womanhood with thoughts like, *I need to be rescued by a man* (thoughts from which, I suppose, we need to be rescued by feminist psychologists). Perhaps, to some extent, they are right. But how do you explain little boys and *their* worship of superheros? Seems to me both sexes dream of being rescued by a larger-than-life benevolent being.

Children realize early on that no mere mortal can save them from the evil forces in this world. The rescuer, the hero, the *savior* must be of supernatural stock. Is it coincidence that Jesus Christ so perfectly fulfills this childhood longing? (A longing that never, even in adulthood, really goes away.) The Book of the Revelation is, for the good guys, the ultimate fairy tale come true. Our Hero, the Royal Son, will come riding in on a white horse to rescue us from the evil dragon and take us to live happily ever after with Him—in a jeweled city of no more tears. Talk about the fulfillment of every child's fantasy. But while I wait along with boys and girls for my Heavenly Prince to come, I've been given the privilege of living with an average, everyday human hero.

Enter Scott.

From the moment I met my husband-to-be, I could tell he had the raw makings of a hero. Of course, in fantasy, it's romantic to be in love with a man who leans toward the heroic and adventure-esque. In reality, it's terrifying. There's not space to cover the Epic Adventures of Scott Man—so how about I lightly touch on the last six months?

Let's see, there was the day Scott was supposed to come home early to watch the kids while I went to a class. He breezed in about thirty minutes late, rushed me off, and offered no explanation for his tardiness. The next morning, over a leisurely cup of coffee, Scott mentioned—almost as an aside—why he had been late the night before. Seems he'd been helping a woman get her head together—literally.

The woman of which he spoke had been in a car accident near the bridge Scott crosses on his daily commute home. Our hero was first on the scene.

"So," Scott calmly related, "I crawled into the cab of the woman's pickup. The skin across the top of her head had split in two when it hit the windshield, exposing her skull. So I held the two flaps of skin together and put pressure on the wound with my shirt until the paramedics got there."

"And you call *this* an excuse for being late?" I teased, amazed he actually kept this story to himself overnight. "Is she going to be OK?"

"Well, it took some talking to calm her down, but I think she's going to be fine."

Now, I don't know about you, but if I had been in my husband's place, I would have found this turn of events incredibly newsworthy. As a matter of fact, as I told Scott, "If I had been the one to help that woman close her wound—shoot, if I'd Band-aid-ed someone's *paper cut*—I would have been tooting my own horn even as I pulled up into the driveway!"

Not so with my husband. He is understatement personified—which is, I suppose, the sign of a true hero. Strong. Quiet. Modest. A man of steel with just the right mixture of compassion. The sort of hero all little girls want to marry when they grow up.

Then there was this past summer with Scott, the Olympic Mountain Man. While on a business trip with my publishers in Denver, I let Scott off the "husband hook" for the day to do whatever he wanted—with assurances from him that he'd make it back in time for dinner with friends. True to his word, Scott met me at our hotel door just in time for dinner, though I noticed he was a little out of breath.

It wasn't until hours later, after the dinner, that I asked my husband for details on how he'd whiled away the afternoon.

"Oh," he answered nonchalantly, "I climbed to the top of the highest mountain in the Rockies."

"Come again?" I asked, blinking.

"Yeah," he continued, "I knew I didn't have much time, so I just started running up Mount Elbert. Without a coat or hiking boots or gear or anything, I figured I could make some good time."

"Wait," I stammered. "You hiked up a mountain without a coat? In your tennis shoes? No water, no food, no backpack, no emergency kit?"

"Yeah, it was kind of stupid I guess," he admitted. "Before long, I sort of felt like I was living through the ol' Pony Express motto. I ran through rain, then sleet, then snow. All I missed was the black of night. But it was kind of funny, too."

"Oh?"

"Yeah, when I reached the crest of the mountain, these two ice climbers coming from the glacier side reached the top at exactly the same time I did. They were dressed from head to toe in these huge Eskimo parkas, loaded down with climbing gear. Anyway, they just sort of peeked up over the side of the cliff as the snow swirled around them. And there I was in a summer shirt, standing in the middle of a blizzard on top of this mountain. All they could do was stare."

"No kidding."

"So I said, 'I guess this is the top.' They just kept staring, and then, finally, they sort of grunted. Then I said, 'You know, I'm not really dressed for this. I best be moseying along.'"

I shook my head and asked, "So, Mountain Man, how long did all this take you?"

"The whole trip, up and back only took a total of three hours and forty-five minutes. The guide at the bottom couldn't believe it."

"Scott, I can't believe you cut it that close!" I shouted incredulously. "You *had* to believe you'd make record time if you were going to keep your promise to me."

He looked at me thoughtfully as he brushed back his sandy blond hair with his fingers. "Yeah," he answered slowly, "guess I did."

Keep in mind, Scott reported all this in the tone of voice he uses for telling me he had the tuna on whole wheat for lunch.

Let's fast-forward now to as recently as a month ago. While our family was eating dinner, I happened to mention that I'd seen a huge garbage truck laying on its side in front of a local store.

"Oh, yeah," Scott said, taking a bite of his salad, "that happened right in front of me. This morning on my way to work, I climbed on top of the truck and helped pull the driver out."

"Oh, sure, Scott," I prodded. "Come on—this 'hero thing' is getting to be a bit much."

He just looked at me and shrugged as if to say, "I can't help it. I only do what must be done." Scott the Rescue Man, doing his good deed for the morning.

A mere two weeks ago, my husband strolled in the front door reeking of smoke. He headed to the freezer and made an ice pack, placing it between his blistered hands. His face looked as though he'd spent a week on the beach without sunscreen.

"So what have you been doing now?" I asked, inspecting his wounds. "Fighting fires?"

Again, he looked at me with those soulful brown eyes and nodded the nod of a little boy who's been into mischief. Scott had been driving along the road, minding his own business, when, he said, "I saw—off to the side—an older man in a panic. He'd been burning trash, and the flames had leaped out of the trash can and quickly spread to the dry grass and nearby trees. So I stopped my truck and ran out to lend a hand, and that's when I realized the flames were heading straight for the man's home."

You got it. Until the fire department arrived, Scott fought the fire back from the house by shoveling dirt on the flames. Scott, the Volunteer Fire Fighter.

I could go on and on with this man's adventures, both serious and frivolous. For a lark, while we were in Florida, Scott took the kids' dare and bungee-jumped. But no, he couldn't jump straight down like every other daring tourist. He had to do a triple back-flip on the way down. Scott the Man Who Can Leap from Tall Buildings in Three Backward Bounds.

We got a Christmas card last week from people I've never heard of, inviting us to come visit them anytime we might pass through Missouri. Curious, I asked my husband what it was about.

"Oh, yes," Scott said when he saw the card, "those must be the folks whose car broke down awhile back. They were from out of town and had some elderly relatives in the car with them, so I towed them to a service station. Nice people." Scott, the Good Samaritan.

As you know (but it bears repeating), sometimes it scares me to death living with an adventure/rescue-type guy. In all honesty, Scott could easily lose his life someday in the pursuit of a thrill or in trying to help someone. But the truth of the matter is, I married exactly the sort of man I've dreamed about since I was a little girl. And would I stay as fascinated with a book worm, computer nerd, or fellow couch potato? As things are, I got my Hercules, Tarzan, and Prince Charming all rolled up in one.

Oh, there's just one more heroic feat of Scott's I'd like to mention before I sign off and go join my husband (who's currently snoring away in our bed under his cape). Every holiday season my husband dresses up in full Santa Claus regalia and visits a school full of underprivileged children. Then he holds more than 150 of them, one at a time, on his lap while they whisper their most fervent Christmas wishes into his ear.

This year Scott was stretched to superhuman endurance. The day my husband was scheduled to don his costume of thick velvet and fur, we had one of those crazy Texas December heatwaves. The thermometer climbed to nearly 80 degrees. Ho, ho, ho, HOT! But this Santa would not be stopped. One hundred and fifty sweaty lap-sittings later, Scott the Santa Man came home exhausted but jolly. I greeted him with a hug at the door.

"So, Santa, how'd it go?" I asked, motioning for him to sit down while I went to the kitchen for some refreshments.

Scott heaved a sigh as he lowered himself into a recliner and answered, "Great."

"Well, Mr. Santa," I said, handing him a cookie and a glass of milk, "now that I have you all to myself, there's something I've been wanting to tell you for a very long time." I moved to his lap and then whispered in his ear, "Thank you for the pouffy blue princess dress you gave me when I was five. And I also want you to know I finally married myself a real, genuine hero."

"Well, little girl," my Santa-Hero replied, "I have a secret to tell you, too."

"What's that?" I asked, smiling mischievously as I playfully fingered his white fur collar.

"At least two of the children who sat on my lap today wet right on the spot where you're sitting."

I jumped up right away.

But I ask you, honestly, does a man get any more heroic than this?

Many times you have miraculously rescued
me . . . You have been loving and kind to me.
PSALM 18:50, TLB

❧

Why Can't Everybody
Just Play Nice?

Not all of childhood is sweetness and light.
Especially if you are the new kid in school. Or if you wear glasses—glasses so large and round that kids joke about your giant "fly eyes." Or if your front teeth come in with brown indentions instead of pearly white enamel because of some medicine a doctor prescribed when you were an infant.

Childhood is not sweet when it is important to be athletic and you, most definitely, are not. Even if you can hang from a chin-up bar for a hundred hours, it is of no use if you can only manage to throw the softball twenty feet. Without a good throwing arm you cannot receive the Presidential Physical Fitness Award. And that means you not only become a disgrace to the entire physically fit fourth grade, but also to the president of the United States of America.

Childhood is not light when you have a really pretty voice and love to sing, but the music teacher only notices the popular, loudish-singing girls. It is also not fair when that teacher handpicks the cast for the school musical instead of holding open tryouts.

Childhood is not sweet or light when your last name is Arnold and one of the most popular characters on TV is a pig from "Green Acres" named Arnold Ziffel.

Then there was PE. Maybe it's no coincidence that recess sounds a lot like *abscess.* I find them equally enjoyable. I have too many memories of standing against a brick wall, breaking out in a cold sweat, and praying that some preadolescent captain would choose me before I fell victim to the torturous fate of being— horrors—the last one picked.

How about lunch? Or not. I tried to spend as many lunching minutes as possible hiding out in the bathroom to avoid the popular girls' favorite game: Who Does and Does Not Get to Sit by Me? Sweetness and light? Ha!

It was during those middle grade school years I learned that the safest route to survival for me was to pretend to be shy. Better to be nothing, to disappear, than to chance public humiliation by reaching out and being labeled a nerd for daring.

It didn't take long to uncover the fact that fourth through sixth grade girls can be carnivorous, eating each other alive to maintain their place on top of the food chain. Because of that fact, I also learned what it's like to spend some part of every day either fighting back or succumbing to tears, trying to gather the emotional strength to face the next school day's onslaught.

There were those times I couldn't contain it, and would find myself overflowing into my mother's arms. She comforted. She agonized with me. Yet there was little she could say but "I understand" and "I think you're beautiful" and "It will get better" and all the other things we count on mothers to say at such times. It was a horrible, trapped period of life and I, the female embodiment of Charlie Brown, felt sentenced to Grade School Prison.

But somewhere in those miserable years I said to myself, "If I survive this, if I ever get the chance to be pretty or popular, I will find others who are shy and wear glasses and get teased and I will stand by their side and say, 'See these kids here—they are my friends and I happen to think they're pretty cool. Oh, and by the way, they, and anyone else who cares to join in, are welcome to sit by me at lunch.'"

The summer before my first year in junior high, the miracle occurred.

It began when my parents—God bless them—took me to the optometrist, shelling out a wad of hard-earned money I'm sure. I came home squinting and glorying in my new contact lenses—forever free of ol' Fly Eyes! Then it seemed almost overnight that my figure began to curve in and out in all the right places. To complete the transformation, our family dentist painted the brown spots on my teeth with a new white wonder called "bonding." I could smile again—a great big open-mouthed smile.

For the grand occasion of the first day of seventh grade, my mom made me a "knock 'em dead" dress. Its sleeveless green bodice was crisscrossed all over with cheerful strips of white rickrack, and from an empire waist flowed a skirt in the perfect shade of a ripe watermelon. Over the summer, my olive skin had baked to a golden brown and my hair had grown dark and long—long enough to tie into pigtails with thick lengths of matching yarn. For the final touch, I smoothed a tinted gloss over my lips—my first hint of makeup.

On that bright September morning, I had the heady experience of knowing I looked *quite* a picture. I would have known it even if my daddy hadn't given me a mixed look of worry and admiration as I strolled out the front door toward the waiting world of junior high.

Junior high, for me, gradually ushered in a time of "all things new." Boys who once taunted me turned into admirers. Even the popular girls became civil. I found myself growing confident. Then my self-esteem gained a foothold on even more solid ground. I discovered I had value, not only because my parents said I was a great kid, but because I'd discovered that the God who created everything in the whole world loved me. He even gave His life for me—*me*, Becky Arnold, a speck of preteen flesh down here on planet Earth. How can I begin to express the impact this knowledge had on this awkward girl in her season of blooming? (Youth workers take note. Your life and your message of hope make a *difference*.)

Blossoming though I was, I never forgot my "lonesome lunch-room" resolve. I set out to notice the lost, the different, the lonely, dotting our school's crowded halls and lunchrooms. So it came to pass that during my junior high years, and on until I graduated from high school, I befriended the loners, nerds, dorks, dweebs, geeks, freaks, brains, foreign students, artsy-drama types, budding philosophers, "Jesus freaks," and one talk-ative Jewish kid. (The Jewish boy even sent me a telegram from Israel on my wedding day!)

Funny, now that I think about it, I've always preferred the company of those who are a little out of step, a little quirky, a little apart from the popular core. I simply find them more fas-cinating. So I have to confess that my desire to befriend the odd-guy-out wasn't completely altruistic; I have a built-in affinity for those who cha-cha to the beat of a different drum. (Note to my dearest friends: Yes, I'm sorry, but it is true. In some way, you *are* slightly odd. But remember, I love you more for it.)

By the time I reached high school, several girls and I ended up in a loosely formed group. Not a clique really, because we wel-comed anybody and everybody. Two or three times a week we'd walk to my house during our school lunch break. My mother—grateful, I think, for the happy appearance of chit-chatty laugh-ter in my life—put up with the mess and allowed us to freely forage her clean kitchen for snacks. Not only did I begin to form wonderful friendships during those days, but other grade school wounds found their healing during my high school years. (Yes, moms. Yes, suffering eighth graders—there is life after junior high.)

In spite of my less-than-loudish musical beginnings, I went on to join a choir, perform in ensembles, sing solos, and play major parts in school musicals. Unfortunately, I had less luck keeping my name from being associated with pigs and hogs.

My grand stage debut was as the character Moon Beam McSwine, from *L'il Abner*. My part required that I carry a rubber pig in my arms, walk center stage, and belt out, "Howdy, boys, I'm Moon Beam McSwine. Sleeping out with pigs is my line. The fellas admire me, but they won't squire me unless the weather is fine. But I does all right when the wind blows the other way." Enchanting, wasn't it?

In spite of my piggish preamble, the "fellas" indeed seemed to admire me—especially at dress rehearsal when I donned my skimpy hillbilly costume. Thus attired, I encouraged such admiration, in fact, that my mother took no time in sewing extra rows of ruffles to my shorts and neckline before opening night.

And how can I forget that opening night? Unbeknownst to me, as I scooted across the stage for my big entrance, a pair of pantyhose adhered itself to the heel of my foot. The stage hands tried unsuccessfully to catch me, but they were too doubled over with laughter to be of help. The audience laughed and hooted and I ate it up—even after my eyes focused and I discovered it was my pantyhose trail, more than my comedic song, that had them going. Oh, I'll go ahead and say it: It was the night Miss McSwine discovered she had some ham.

For me, this pantyhose event marked a transformation: Rather than shrinking in shame, I found myself laughing along with the rest of them. Liz Curtis Higgs, a fantastic humorist and sweet friend, often says in her talks, "The day we learn to laugh at ourselves is the day we begin to grow up." After years of introspective pain, I was finally on my way.

Besides the joy of uncovering the funny streak buried in my "shy" personality, in my tenth grade year I fell head-over-heels-and-pantyhose in love. Finding a soulmate in Scott left me with a general feeling of "the world is all aglow." I pretty much floated throughout my remaining years in school. In fact, I was so crazy in love that I doubled up on my classes during my junior year and graduated early to become Scott's bride. (See *Marriage 9-1-1* for the rest of *that* story.)

Looking back on it now I have to say that even though my school days ended on a high note, the years of pain left a couple of scars. To this day, my idea of a nightmare is having to "mingle" in a large crowd of people I don't know. Give me one on one, or a small group of new folk, and I'm in my element. But when I'm thrown into an unfamiliar situation where I am supposed to mix and mingle, tears often involuntarily spring to my eyes. I'll find myself, as if on autopilot, escaping to the bathroom or to a quiet spot outside where I can regroup alone. My personal theory is that these emotions are flashbacks to lunchroom days when I stood gazing at a sea of kids, afraid of what to say and wondering where I should sit and if I'd be accepted or rejected.

Yet it's important to note that scars aren't all bad. They serve as reminders of battles endured and of what we want to avoid in the future. I'm not sure I would trade those painful early experiences for easier ones even if I had the power to do so, for they graced my teenage years and adulthood with a heightened sensitivity to feelings of others. I believe the hard experiences in life often leave us kinder people than we would have been if all of childhood was pure sweetness and light.

As a sophomore, singing in a girls' chorus, we performed a beautiful poem by William Penn, set to music. Even then, the words struck a chord in my heart and have followed me all these years.

> I expect to pass through life but once.
> If therefore, there be any kindness I can show . . .
> let me do it now, and not defer or neglect it,
> as *I shall not pass this way again.*

We are given one, and only one, journey through this life. One chance to show affection. One life to give love. I often visualize the faded image of a little girl with thick glasses sitting all alone, her heart aching for friends and a bit of human kindness. Perhaps those of us who've warmed benches and been passed over for others more beautiful try a little harder to love the unlovely. Having experienced the sting of rejection, I now have a tremendous appreciation for those who honor me with their kindness—who add to my everyday humdrum life a touch of sweetness and light.

Today was a great example. I went to our small-town grocery store and was immediately greeted by several of my buddies who work there. Maybe it was because it's the beginning of the Christmas season and I'm feeling especially sentimental; but it suddenly touched me just how special it is to walk into a store where I'm known by name—where small kindnesses have been shared over the years until our over-the-counter experiences have turned into store-bound friendships.

I've come to love Robert, the mentally challenged bag boy who never fails to greet me with a hearty welcome like, "You sure look nice today, ma'am." This, even when I'm wearing my old faded sweats. I know he loves to help, so whenever I can't find an item I ask for Robert's assistance. Then he cheerfully escorts me down the aisle, triumphantly pointing to the desired product on the shelf and shouts, "There it is! You didn't know where it was, huh? Well, I sure found it for you, didn't I? Yep. There it is, right there, yes sirree." It's nice to be helped with such enthusiasm.

I also love the way Judy, my friend and checkout woman, hollers her series of run-on questions in my direction over the heads of other customers.

"Hey, Beck, howyadoin' girl? What've you been up to? Haven't seen you lately." It's nice to be missed.

Small-town kindness. Big-hearted acceptance. How could anyone ever take these things for granted? They couldn't. Not if they'd ever been without.

The highlight of today's trip to the supermarket was being escorted to my car by my favorite stocker. He is up in years; I'm guessing mid-seventies. Over the years, he and I have shared lots of small talk over bags of groceries. After his wife died, he took this job so that he could be around people.

This morning my grocery buddy sensed I was feeling embarrassed about my old station wagon, so he said, "Hey now, don't say anything bad about a good car like this. You need to hang on to it—it'll be a classic someday." He said it with such sincerity, I almost believed him.

As I ducked into the front seat and prepared to put my key in the ignition, I said, "Thank you for the pep talk and for unloading the groceries."

"Oh, you're welcome," he replied, "my pleasure."

But before I could shut the door I noticed my friend standing nearby, hands resting on the empty cart as if there was still something he wanted to say. I smiled up at him and our eyes met.

"And—*Merry Christmas,* Mrs. Freeman!" he said with heartfelt sincerity.

I returned the season's greetings in kind, but he had another gift for me. Something incredible. Something spontaneous. Something purely brimming over with kindness. He walked around the empty cart, over to my car door, ducked down, and gave me a terrific bear hug. I left the grocery store—the *grocery store,* mind you—feeling as though I'd been to a family reunion. And the little girl inside me, the lonely one with big round glasses, smiled clear down to her toes.

I drove home on air, happily stuck in a state of childlike wonder. And as I drove, I thought, *In a perfect world, a kind world, this would be the way a child would feel all the time: chock plumb full of "sweetness and light."*

Be ye kind one to another, tenderhearted.
EPHESIANS 4:32, KJV
❧

Come Watch Our Show!

I recently stopped by for a backporch visit with our neighbor, Mary Sue Gantt, and during the course of our conversation she asked, "Have I ever told you about the first time I ever laid eyes on Gabe?" I wasn't quite sure I really wanted to hear this story, but she continued anyway.

"Well," she said, settling into a lawn chair, "I was taking a walk along the road, when suddenly this little boy pops out of nowhere from a nearby field, grabs my hand, and says, 'Come on!' Before I could even think, he led me down to the edge of the lake. Then he plopped down on his stomach by the bank and ducked his entire head under water."

"That's my Gabe."

"That's not all. Then he lifted up his head, the water pouring in streams from his bangs, and hollered up at me, 'I learned how to duck my head under water today! Idn't that great?'"

Mary Sue said she thought it was terrific, indeed, and she and Gabe have been buddies ever since.

What struck me about that story was Gabe's attitude. He was not only excited about his newfound skill; he assumed others would, of course, want to see him perform it. Why wouldn't they? What happens between childhood and adulthood to dampen this natural assumption that we will succeed—what quiets our enthusiasm?

Zachary burst into our bedroom the other night with a story he swore was true, and it is a perfect example of the way many of us begin thinking as we move into adulthood, always futurizing worst-case scenarios. According to my son, there was a woman sitting in her car in a grocery store parking lot in Houston, Texas. Her head was resting against the steering wheel. A passerby observed that the woman seemed to be in distress, so he opened her car door and asked, "Ma'am, are you all right?"

"No," she replied feebly, "I've been shot in the back of the head. I think I feel a bit of my brains on my shoulder."

Of course the man wasted no time in calling 9-1-1. When the paramedics arrived on the scene, they immediately began checking the woman's vital signs, careful not to move her unnecessarily. That done, the paramedic drew a breath and asked, "Ma'am, what makes you think you've been shot?"

She repeated her tale weakly. "I felt something explode against the back of my head and I can feel some of my brains on my shoulder."

"Miss," drawled the paramedic with a grin, "what you've got on your shoulder is a canned biscuit. Looks like a whole can of them shot open from the grocery sack in the back of your car."

This was one of the funniest stories I'd ever heard, and I love to tell it to crowds of women. Who among us hasn't wondered if our headache might actually be a fast-growing tumor? Imagining worst-case scenarios is every mother's specialty.

As you now know, I spent my grade school years feeling like a little turtle—terrified to stick my head out of the shell. (Never, in my wildest moments, would I have dreamed of plunging it under water in front of a stranger!) But, thankfully, I had a cousin who shared Gabe's enthusiastic outlook on life. And she would pull me "onstage" with her now and then, without giving me a chance to say no.

My cousin, Jamie, was tall and lanky, and she wore her flaxen tresses pulled back in a yard-long ponytail braid. She also wore braces on her teeth, which she despised. But what I remember most about Jamie is that she was a royal hoot. She was the embodiment of Pippi Longstocking, almost a fantasy character who leaned toward eccentricity, always game for any adventure, and hovering about her, an air of supreme goodheartedness.

No matter what awkward stage I happened to be passing through, Jamie never swayed in verbalizing her high opinion of me. She told me I was pretty and smart and funny and talented. And whenever I got a chance to go visit my cousin, I felt all those things might, indeed—at least for the week—be true. Odd thing about human nature: It's not only how charming our *friends* are that causes us to love them, it's how delightful they make us *feel* when we're with them.

I arrived at Jamie's house an unassuming little thing; but soon after stepping into her world, I felt more like a star about to be born. I barely had time to throw my suitcase on Jamie's chenille bedspread before she grabbed a pencil and paper and began writing out our schedule.

"OK," Jamie said, chewing on the eraser, "the first thing I think we ought to do is put on a dance show." Her assurance was so contagious that I had no time for self-doubt or contemplating whether or not I had what it takes to perform. From Jamie's way of looking at it, *of course* we had talent—why waste it? Never mind that I'd never shuffle-ball-changed a step in my life. We simply had to get on with the show and give out whatever it was we had to the waiting world. As a matter of fact, Jamie explained that she had only just yesterday given dancing a whirl.

"Nothing to it," she assured me. Within an hour or so, Jamie had not only taught me to dance (admittedly it was mostly arm-waving, high-kicking, and twirling-around-and-arounding), but she'd gathered up an audience of little brothers and sisters and parents and neighborhood children—and charged them a quarter each to watch our show. In that one week, we also put on a magic show, drew portraits, performed roadside slapstick routines, held a gymnastics tournament, made cream puffs from a gourmet cookbook, and became accomplished beauticians (meaning that, armed with rat-tail combs and industrial-strength hairspray, we teased every inch of each other's hair into enormous balls of fuzz.)

I owe Jamie a lot. Not only were so many of my best child-hood memories sweetened by her presence as a friend, she taught me what Gabriel seems to have been given from birth: the ability to *assume* one can learn a new skill, *assume* it will probably work out well, and *assume* others will enjoy watching the performance. And finally, to assume it will be more fun than—well, more fun than spontaneous head dunking!

One of my favorite speakers in the Dallas area is Susie Hum-phreys. Susie delivers a delightful talk entitled, "I Can *Do* That!" From her youngest days, with little education and no experience, Susie assumed her way from one fantastic job to another. One of her life's mottos is, "Volunteer it! You can learn it later!" The world is starving for more Gabes, more Jamies, more Susies, (and a few less Biscuit Brains).

August, 1995. Family Reunion. Houston, Texas.

Jamie strolls out into the sun from the open door, her arms open wide. Flowing mane of blond hair. Perfect straight white teeth. A figure I thought only came manufactured in Barbie Doll Dream Houses. Tan, dimples. Where, I wonder, did Pippi Longstocking go?

Not to worry, the heart of Pippi is still here—only now she's a little harder to detect under Jamie's startling beauty. But not for long. We are immediately both shocked and pleased to dis-cover we own the same model car—both of us have been chauf-feuring our four kids around our respective towns in old Buick station wagons. Yes, hers even has faded contact paper wood-grain siding like Sag's! We wonder aloud how many thirty-something women, besides ourselves, drive the same gas guzzlers our mothers drove in the seventies?

Suddenly Jamie remembers a story.

"Oh, Becky," she laughs, "can you believe I was stopped by a policeman awhile back, in that station wagon, for *weaving* on the road?"

My mouth drops open. I can't believe there's yet another coincidence. "Weaving?" I ask, my voice growing louder and more excited. "You've been stopped for weaving? *I've just been stopped* for weaving, too!" It is a touching moment. Like finding a long lost twin. I finish my story.

"The most embarrassing thing about it was that when the officer asked if I'd been drinking, Gabriel looked at the Coke I'd been sipping and assured him I *had been!*"

But Jamie can match this. She speaks with great animation, her slim hands flying to emphasize the highlights of her story.

"Listen: The policeman asked me if I knew, while I was weaving, I'd also been speeding. My little Jacob piped up, too, just like Gabe. He looked straight at the officer and said, 'Oh, yes. My mom *did* know she was going too fast. I've been telling her to slow down for miles and miles. Even stuck my arm out the window a ways back there and the wind nearly took it off!'"

Jamie and I laugh so hard we are leaning on each other's arms for support. We cannot believe we've both raised sons who will freely tattle on their *own mothers* to strangers in uniform. I cherish the kinship of laughter we've shared over the years, the music of little-girl giggles echos in my memory. And I realize, suddenly, that Jamie is my oldest friend and how special it is to share nearly forty years of history with her. A quote by John Leonard plays about my mind: "It takes a long time to grow an old friend."

Goodness knows Jamie cannot let our good stories go to waste. She's already pulling me by the sleeve toward the kitchen, urging, "Becky, come on. We've got to tell this to . . ." And once again, I've no time for self-doubt or wondering if I have the ability to perform. Jamie's sure enough for the both of us. After all, we have some great stuff to share; why waste it? So I smooth my shirt, stand a little taller, smile a little wider, and get ready to follow Jamie "on stage"—to give out whatever it is we've got to the waiting world. Or at least to our parents and brothers and sisters and aunts and uncles milling about in the kitchen.

And this time, we do not even charge them a quarter.

If you love someone you will . . . always believe
in him, always expect the best of him.
1 CORINTHIANS 13:7, TLB

࿇

I Can't Wait 'Til Camp!

L ast summer, in East Texas, I drove Sag through a set of iron gates (thankfully, they *were* open) and cruised down a black-topped road. Just as I rounded a curve I encountered a large animal. The beast had planted itself in the middle of the road, and there it stood, methodically chewing its cud. Having grown accustomed to life outside the big city, I wasn't all that shocked to come upon a hoofed, cud-chewing animal sunning itself in the center of traffic. But this was a bovine of a different color. This creature had a hump on its back, and its legs rose to the top of my station wagon. It was a camel—of the Arabian desert variety.

The dromedary began eyeing my hood ornament hungrily and licking his chops in anticipation. Not knowing what to do, I honked the horn. All I got in response was the nonchalant blink of his ebony eyes. He would not be moved. *What? Had I thought he could be honked into action like some common Hereford or Jersey?*

Just then a long-legged cowboy strode by and tossed out some advice.

"I'd go around him if I was you. He's fixin' to spit."

And so I did. Speedily in fact, and—may I add—none too soon. Welcome to Jan-Kay Ranch—Detroit, Texas.

I came to this unusual setting to bring Rachel and her two girl-friends for a week of summer camp. Gabe tagged along for the ride. However, when he saw the camel, and then the llamas, ante-lopes, wild pigs, peacocks, monkeys—and of course, the tiger, bear, and baby elephant—it was all too much. How dare I bring him this close to Paradise only to take him home again?

What is a good, sensible mother to do in such situations? I haven't the foggiest. I only know that this mother ended up leav-ing her son at camp with a plastic bag full of clothes scrounged from the recesses of her station wagon.

Honestly, I knew Gabe would be fine at this family-owned camp. I went to this very same ranch with the junior high group from my church. The wild and exotic animals weren't around back then, but the cabins and rec hall and lake were exactly as I'd remembered them.

I had loved those church camp weeks at Jan-Kay Ranch. I loved watching the early morning mist rise over the lake as white-washed egrets flew from stump to fish and back again. I recall spir-itual stirrings inside, as I read from Scriptures that were just begin-ning to make sense. I found, lying between those pages, fascinating situations involving what I now call "Camelots of the Soul"—stories where truth, goodness, mercy, and *right* stood its ground in the midst of cruelty, jealousy, confusion, and wrong. It was refreshing. I found myself, as a teenager, especially hungry for such shining visions. (One doesn't find many shining visions in the daily halls of public school.)

I also remember the beating of my heart as I stepped out of my cabin on summer evenings, just-showered and sweet-smelling after a day filled with team games and noise and sweat. I can almost hear the screen door bouncing closed behind me with its rhythmic thump, and feel the adolescent hoping-beyond-hope that a cute boy might walk by the porch, take notice, and smile in my direction. Evening hayrides. Midnight gossip. Morning walks. Afternoon swims.

Nice memories. Very nice.

About five years ago, I was invited back to Jan-Kay Ranch to attend a women's retreat. I rediscovered the mist and the lake, unchanged and serene. On this stay there would be no boys to impress, however. The boys had turned into husbands—*our husbands,* who were graciously staying home with our children so we could escape for a weekend. And we women had come, hoping to rediscover a bit of spiritual Camelot in the midst of our hectic, modern lives. Along with absorbing the Scriptures for their goodness and truth, we also played and yakked and laughed and ate goodies until the wee hours. To get to Camelot, m'lady, there needs be some fun along the way.

Seriously, every woman should have a chance to go back to camp again. For one thing, it's great for the ego to see other gorgeous, sophisticated women without their makeup, dressed in flannel feety pajamas. It has a way of bringing high church ladies down to my comfort level. With the makeup removed, masks also drop with more ease, and the resulting gab sessions can be the best. I, for one, didn't want to miss out on any late-night, impromptu round circles.

One night during the retreat, way past midnight, I was plagued with bunk-bed insomnia. Feeling slumber-partyish anyway, I climbed down from my perch and pulled a plate of brownies from my food stash. I was a woman on a mission. Confident I could find another night owl, I walked out into the darkness seeking a friend with whom I could share a chocolate conversation.

Without my contact lenses, it was a terrific challenge to feel my way through the blackness. Finally, I spotted a lone figure sitting on the front porch in the moonlight. I walked toward the woman, sat down beside her, looked up at the starry night, and said dreamily, "Isn't it beautiful out here? I guess you couldn't sleep either, huh? Listen—I come bearing gifts. Would you like a fudge brownie?"

There was no answer. The woman sat stone still, staring straight ahead. *Oh, great,* I thought, *she must have wanted to be alone.* But as I looked closer, I jumped back with a start. The figure was not a woman after all. I'd just offered my brownies to a wooden Indian.

As I rose to find more lively companionship, I patted the Indian's knee and offered him some free advice—"Fella, you really should loosen up." The incident was a big hit when I finally found a live, nocturnal audience to share my brownies with.

As much fun as it is to fellowship, there *is* one big drawback to camp: All camp directors seem to insist on organizing some form of physical group activity. It conjures images of that ugly childhood word: recess. And you know how I feel about *that*. After what happened at one retreat, though, I now like it even less. But, still, I know it's good for my character to be stretched beyond my comfort zone every once in a while.

The fateful physical activity to which I'm referring had ominous overtones from the start. The idea was for us ladies to participate in what is called a Ropes Course—a series of challenges involving wood and ropes and needlessly frightening tests designed to help bond a team together (from sheer terror, I assume).

The nightmare of tests is the trust fall. At this juncture in the course, each of us had to ascend a four-feet-high platform. Then we, being adults of sane mind, were to fall backwards—one at a time—from that height into the locked and waiting hands of our fellow middle-aged, baggy-armed comrades. I learned one thing from that experience. Peer pressure doesn't ever completely loosen its grip, even in midlife. To chants of, "Don't be a sissy, Becky," I climbed, I fell, they caught, it hurt like the dickens.

When it was my turn to join the "catchers," I was relieved. "Better to be a catcher than a fall guy," I always say. The next woman to climb the platform was rather large. When she plummeted, we did our best to break her fall, but down to the ground she went with a sickening thud. Stunned, the fallen woman shook her head as if to clear it. Then she uttered the bravest words ever spoken by a mere mortal.

"I want to try it again," she said. I couldn't believe it. We'd just dropped this woman, our friend, on a *trust* fall, for goodness sake. We had just proven we were not the sort to be trusted. But she believed in us, and she believed in herself. As our fearless faller began her climb, I locked arms with the woman across from me.

She whispered to me under her breath, "Becky, if you let go, I'll kill you. We have to make this catch."

Our Lady of Bravery, ready for her descent, stood on the platform and turned slowly around. She fell straight back, arms folded across her chest. We caught her! Hallelujah! (And it hurt!) But the whole experience resulted in a new hero added to my own personal vision of Camelot. In my eyes, this brave woman became a true knight in shining armor, for she was determined to see our ragtag group rise to the challenge. And even though we failed her once, she was willing to sacrifice her own body, King Arthur style, so our faith in each other could be restored.

Having learned such a significant moral lesson, I limped back to my cabin, warm with emotion. I had forced myself to experience the ultimate camp challenge—I had been part and parcel of a team's success, and I had to admit it was a good feeling. Wild horses couldn't drag me into doing a Ropes Course *again*—for I am now officially at the end of my ropes—but I'm proud to say, "I did it."

These types of experiences make up an unforgettable week of camp: conquering challenges, teamwork, beautiful scenery, nature's animals, late-night talks, spiritual refreshment, chocolate. Mulling it over, I knew that Gabe would be a natural for summer camp—even with nothing but a plastic bag full of old clothes. As it turned out, I couldn't have been more correct.

I made a mid-week visit to Jan-Kay, carrying fresh clothing rations for my little camper-to-go. Once I made it past the camel guard, and parked my car—hood ornament intact—it didn't take long to locate Gabe. He was happily feeding Eedie the baby elephant fistfuls of popcorn. As I strolled up to say hello, I saw Eedie stretch out her trunk, grab the popcorn bag Gabe was holding and in an instant, gulp it down, paper and all.

Gabe was startled at first and then he got tickled as only little boys can—breaking out in a gale of spontaneous giggles. The scene of Gabe bent over with laughter and the elephant scarfing down his bag of popcorn, went "click" in that place in my head where pictures I don't want to forget are stored. *At moments like this Gabe makes it look like so much fun to be a kid. And if I can't be one, at least it's fun to have one.*

Though he looked as happy as I've ever seen him, I wondered if my baby had suffered any gone-away-to-camp-for-the-first-time homesickness. I'd been reading Art Linkletter's latest edition of *Kids Say the Darndest Things* and had come across a letter written by one little homesick soul trying to keep up a brave-camper front. It read, "Dear Mom and Dad, I am not homesick. Please write to me. Are you coming Sunday? Please come. I need some clean towels. Write and tell me if you are coming. Please come and bring the baby. They keep us so busy here, I don't have time to get homesick. Please come Sunday. Love, Paul. P.S. Next year I think I'll come to camp for the shorter period."

After reading this pitiful letter, I wanted to be especially sensitive to my son in his first extended experience away from home.

"Gabe," I asked gingerly, "have you had any crying spells? At night maybe?"

"Yeah," he answered sheepishly, "last night I did."

I nodded sympathetically and rubbed his back. He continued, a twinge of bittersweet to his voice.

"I cried because camp only lasts for three more days, and I want to stay forever."

That did it. I was convinced. Every kid should get a chance to at least try a wonderful, healthy, eye-opening "camp experience." Especially kids like you and me, who still need excursions in nature, to laugh out loud in surprise, to have our faith refreshed and our friendships deepened—who are, forever and always, in search of whatever bits of Camelot can be found in this hard-edged ol' world.

He satisfies me with good things.
He makes me young again.

PSALM 103:5, NCV

❧

Sorry Boys, This Is Girl Talk

I can no longer remember what my daughter's right ear looks like. As far as I know, she may not even have one anymore. How *could* I possibly know? The ear has been beneath a telephone receiver for at least the last ten months. Not only that, but the telephone cord has transformed into Rachel's umbilical cord—transmitting all the information needed to sustain life in junior high school.

Another interesting phenomenon: I only see my daughter these days as part of a pair. She's always with one of her best friends—namely, Michelle (whom Scott lovingly nicknamed, Miss Prissy) or Cricket (whom Scott insists on calling Grasshopper). I try not to look at the situation as though I've lost a daughter, but rather, as if I've gained a revolving set of twins.

It's imperative, of course, that Rachel and her girlfriends keep up-to-the-minute on the details of every aspect of each other's lives. The following are halves of actual conversations I've heard from Rachel's end of the phone chatter.

"That zit hasn't cleared up? Ohmgosh, how *awful!*"

"He did? He said he liked me? Liked me, like, LIKED me, or liked me, like, *likes* me?"

"Oh, yeah! I spilt Dr. Pepper on my Massomo shirt—*What?* Did I not tell you that?"

"He's the guy that threw a french fry at me in the cafeteria, and then I giggled like a dork and milk started spurting out my nose and I, like, thought I would *die!* You know—he's the one that used to go out with Chelsea, and just broke up with Heather, and I think he's really fine but I just don't know for sure, for *sure* if I'd go out with him or not."

Just as an aside—is any other parent out there stupefied by elementary and junior high kids saying they are "going out" with someone in their class? All I want to know is, where are they going out to? When I ask this question of my children they look at me as if I'm fresh from having my lobotomy done. "MUH-ther! They don't *go* anywhere. It's just what they call it these days."

"And they never actually go out anywhere together?"

"Nope."

"Do they talk to each other, or sit by each other, or hold hands or anything?" I ask naively.

This question always gets great laughs from Gabe. It is obvious that I am a confused old woman, so he explains patiently.

"You see, Mom, if a boy likes a girl, he gets his friend to ask the girl's friend if she wants to go out with him. If she tells her friend to tell his friend yes, then they are going out together. And they don't ever have to talk to each other or nothin' if they don't want to. Then when they get tired of going out, the boy or the girl gives a note to the friend of the other boy or girl saying they don't want to go out with them anymore and that's it! Then they can start all over again."

As my little nephew pointed out, I must be too old to understand—which is scary because it seems like only yesterday I used to be the *daughter* trying to explain what "going *with* someone" meant, to my mom. (I wonder if my mother went through the same conversation trying to explain what "going steady" meant to her mother. I can just hear my grandmother asking, "Going steady? What does that mean, 'going *steady*'? What? Are the rest of us going crooked or rocky or something?")

Perhaps Rachel and I aren't really so far apart. At least I still understand one thing: the need for girl talk. This weekend three of my old girlfriends and I gathered in Dallas and rented a hotel suite for a night. We arrived about 5:00 in the evening and talked and giggled until 2:00 A.M., slept a few hours, rose again at 8:30 the next morning, and continued nonstop chatter until noon when we practically had to pry ourselves away from the hotel. There were still stories untold, discussions left hanging, questions unanswered. My stomach, three days later, is still sore from hours of laughing.

"What in the world did you girls talk about for thirteen straight hours?" Scott asked in amazement when I arrived back home.

"Oh, I don't know," I said. "First, I guess, we told our 'cute kid' stories. Brenda told how she'd bought her little Ben a one-minute timer and told him to brush his teeth until the sand ran out of the hour glass. The next time she passed by the bathroom, Ben had thick foam all around his mouth, dripping all over his chin, his shoulder, and down his right arm. Bless his heart, turns out Brenda gave him a *three-minute* timer. And then Shawn told about her four-year-old decorating the floor of her car with hundreds of doodle bugs while she was napping."

"And this kind of stuff really entertains you girls?"

"Oh, we *love* it!"

"Did you talk about any current events or anything?" Scott asked, trying hard to understand.

"Of course. We discussed nutrition. Did you know that the Cabbage Diet gave someone an ulcer? We decided that diet must work by putting a hole in your stomach so the food can leak out. Then after we finished discussing all the diets we'd been on, we ate strawberries dipped in chocolate."

"Typical females."

"Then we talked about how to make ends meet. Crafts and stuff."

"How fascinating."

"Shawn won top prize with 'how to get whatever you want for pennies, with a bucket of paint.' She's painted her cement floor in her kitchen to look like grass and cobblestone, painted a fireplace on a blank wall—and get this, somebody gave them a white couch but it was all covered with stains so—"

"She didn't!"

"Yes, she *did!* She painted that sucker red with a gallon of water-based enamel!"

"Anything else?"

"Well," I replied, batting my eyelashes. "We talked about our husbands." This perked up Scott's ears.

"So, did you discuss everyone's marital problems?"

"Yes, as a matter of fact we did. But you will be pleased to know that we all decided to keep the men we married."

"Why?"

"Because you guys are so good at understanding us women—and playing Mr. Mom so we can get away now and then for a girls' night out."

I kissed Scott on the cheek. He grinned sheepishly and darted outside to do some man stuff. But before he closed the door I heard him say, "Women! I'll never understand 'em."

I didn't tell Scott that eventually our girl talk turned deeper: We talked of ongoing quests to find our purpose in life, what it means to really know God, to relax and be real. We each wondered if we'd ever overcome the pain of our imperfections as women, mothers, and wives. How could we learn to forgive more, holler less, love our families better? Women do this talking thing really, really well. Connectors R Us.

In contrast, Ray Ortland speaks to groups of males on the topic, "The Loneliness of Men." In a candid moment, so rare among men, Mr. Ortland even admitted that sometimes in rooms full of people he feels like a little kid with his thumb in his mouth, swinging his legs back and forth and wondering,

"What's going on?" Surveys from Promise Keepers reveal how few men, especially pastors, have even one close friend with whom they can be totally honest. This makes my heart ache. It also makes me want to burst into a chorus of "I Enjoy Being a Girl."

Ask any female—from age four to ninety-four—and she will tell you she understands *exactly* what Anne of Green Gables longed for when she said, "I've dreamed of meeting her all my life . . . a bosom friend—an intimate friend, you know—a really kindred spirit to whom I can confide my inmost soul."[4] No place is really home to a woman until she has a friend she can call up for no reason at all.

Scott stands in bewildered amazement as he observes my friendships and those of his blossoming daughter. As a matter of fact, he looks at us both as something almost alien. According to Dee Brestin's book, *The Friendships of Women,* "The friendships between little girls differ from the friendships between little boys."[5] She also points out that perhaps it is not always such a terrible thing, this lack of deep conversation between the males of our species. Some of it may just be a built-in difference between the sexes. Brestin goes on to quote Zick Rubin, author of *Children's Friendships,* as saying, "Girls not only have a much stronger need for friendship than boys, but demand an intensity in those friendships that *boys prefer living without*"[6] (emphasis mine).

Yes! Though my husband and my sons value their friends, they've got to be *doing* something. Conversation is on the side, rarely the main course. None of my three sons' friends call to find out what color socks the other is wearing to school the next day. There are no long chats between the males in our family over hairstyles and the latest school gossip. Hurt feelings between the boys and their friends are almost never a topic of dinner conversation. And frankly, they don't seem to miss it or need it. Yes, my daughter is unique among her brothers. She is in training for womanhood and honing friendships that will, hopefully, stay her over a lifetime. Just as women friends have sustained and nourished her mother and her grandmother, and her great-grandmother before her.

I just got off the phone a few minutes ago. It was Mary, one of my best friends. She said, "Becky, I just made a decision. But I need you to tell me that I'm doing the right thing." I listened to her story and answered her with exactly what she wanted to hear. "Absolutely, Mary. You are doing the right thing." (A man, you see, might want to point out miscellaneous logical options. This, of course, only serves to infuriate a woman.) "Thanks," Mary answered, audibly relieved, "that's all I needed to know."

After I hung up, Scott casually asked what Mary's call was about. I answered, "You wouldn't understand. It was girl talk."

Then I went on to discuss Mary's conversation with the only other person in my family who *would* understand—my daughter, my Rachel.

Some of our women amazed us.
LUKE 24:22
❧

THIRTEEN

Which Way Do I Go Now?

M y husband tells a story to each of our children as they pass
from the gently flowing rivers of childhood into the
treacherous waterfalls of adolescence. It is a story about a friendship—about a fork in the road and about simple choices that
affect us for the rest of our lives.

But first, some background on my husband's foray into teen-
agehood.

The first time I saw Scott, he was fourteen, and I, barely thirteen. I was new to church, new to believing in Christ—new to
everything. It took no time for the youth group to label me: I
was cast as the Goody-Two-Shoes Ding Dong. (Funny how
those teenage labels have such staying power.) I could hardly
wait to go along with my youth group on an outing to the
park—to get to know lots of wholesome kids my age who were
as interested in "higher spiritual things" as I had become. Boy,
was I in for a shock.

The old church bus pulled into the park entrance, and as soon
as the kids unloaded onto the grass, I noticed one adorable guy,
in particular, heading off in the direction of an arching stone

bridge. I mean he was *gorgeous.* Doe-brown eyes. Tom Selleck–style creases along the sides of his wide smile. Perfect, white, straight teeth. Wide shoulders, arms that rippled with muscles—a body built better than any fourteen-year-old's I'd ever seen. And his hair was straight, thick, soft—the kind I would have loved to run my fingers through. That is, if I had not been a Goody-Two-Shoes Ding Dong.

I softly hummed a happy tune, checked to make sure my hair was in place, and meandered off in the direction of the cute boy. When I got to the bridge I gasped, turned around, and whistled off in the opposite direction. For there, beneath the bridge was Adorable Guy and a few other kids from the youth group passing around and guzzling a clear bottled beverage as fast as they could get it down. Adorable Guy, as you've probably guessed by now, was my Scott. And the clear beverage was straight vodka.

The next time I saw Adorable Scott, he was leaning on a rather sturdy girl's shoulder. She took him to the church bus where he promptly threw up all over the floor.

Scott was so ill all he could think about was getting home and into a bed. In the meantime, his parents heard of his adventure in the park. To this day, Scott is grateful for his dad's compassionate, matter-of-fact response to the embarrassing event. Jim (Scott's dad) walked into his son's room, where Scott was writhing from a terrific hangover, and said, "Son, I heard what happened. You know, I think the natural consequences of this are probably worse than anything I could do to you. Sleep it off. We'll talk tomorrow."

The next Sunday morning, the Under-the-Bridge-Drinking-Gang apologized to the entire youth group. Scott cannot speak for the other kids; he only knows his own apology was sincere. He desperately wanted to do what was right.

Sometimes I think I've been a "good girl" all my life (at least in the outward forms of "goodness") because I am a great big chicken. Sure, I'd rather say it was because I had such deep moral fiber that I fended off temptation by sheer courage and character. More truthfully, I was scared to death to "sin." If a TV commercial said that drinking, smoking, or taking drugs was an unhealthy thing to do, that it might could even kill you, I would have been terrified that one puff or one sip would put me six feet under. Those public school anti-smoking, anti-drug campaigns worked like a charm on me.

Scott, being a guy and being less naive about the ways of the world, and realizing early on that grown-ups don't necessarily know everything, was at a higher risk for experimentation.

And it is at this point the story that my husband tells our children begins.

During this "risky" time, Scott met Larry,* a boy his age who was in need of a friend. Scott's mom, unaware of the danger, even encouraged Scott to befriend Larry. He seemed like such a nice, lonely kid.

But Larry, at age fourteen, was already on a slippery path— drugs enticing him to escape from hard reality. For a while, Scott was tempted, too, still fighting the part of him that wanted to be one of the gang, to be cool. Back then, he even went by the nickname "Joe Cool." Often when I saw him around town, Scott would be wearing a striped tank top, a burgundy beret, and sunglasses—and he rode a motorcycle. I mean, he was one cool-looking dude. To keep up this reputation, Scott found himself denying his soul of souls and giving in to the stuff of illusion.

The inward struggle intensified until the day came to make a choice.

One afternoon, Scott and Larry went out riding their motorcycles.

They came to a literal fork in the road—a crossroads. Something clicked in Scott's head. He pulled over to the side of the road, turned off the engine of his motorcycle, and spoke. "Larry," he stammered, searching for words to accurately express what he wanted to say. "Look, I just can't do this."

"Can't do what, man?" Larry asked, his voice heavy and slow.

---

* Not his real name

"I can't go the way you are going. You're heading the wrong direction, Larry, and I'm not going down with you. Look, I'm going to drive over to the youth director's house—you know, that guy from my church—and I'm gonna talk to him. You wanna go with me?"

Larry looked sadly at Scott for a minute and then shook his head. "Do what you have to do, man. I've gotta do what I have to do."

Larry drove off one way; Scott turned in the opposite direction—for a visit with a man he could trust. A man whom Scott knew to have faith, character, courage, conviction—the things that had been knocking at his soul. And just that quickly, in the blink of an eye, the choice had been made.

We cannot deny the fact that some moments in our lives hold more significance than others. We mark the stages, the milestones, in our lives by small turning points. The scene of Larry driving off on his motorcycle is forever imprinted in Scott's mind. The memory marks a moment in time when Scott followed his inner convictions and let the pieces of Joe Cool fall where they may.

The man in Robert Frost's immortal poem, "The Road Not Taken," acknowledges that some moments in time are seconds of such significance, that years from now they will not only be recalled, they will also be *retold*.

> I shall be telling this with a sigh
> Somewhere ages and ages hence:
> Two roads diverged in a wood, and I—
> I took the one less traveled by,
> And that has made all the difference.

In time, Scott would realize more profoundly the full impact of his choice.

From that afternoon on, Larry took a fast ride toward darkness, deluded by the fog of revolving drugs into believing he was heading toward light. Larry had a precious praying mother, and God intervened time and again, but Larry always continued to make one disastrous choice after another.

Years passed, and every so often Larry would ride up on his motorcycle and shoot the breeze with Scott. Larry had plenty of drug buddies, but he knew Scott had been the closest thing to a true friend he would ever have. Scott lost count of the times he offered to get Larry some help. Finally, Scott gave up trying, and when Larry came by he just tried to be kind, to be a friend in the middle of all the darkness.

More years went by and Scott married me, and we had our first baby boy—Zachary. Life was good, the sun shone bright, we had moved into a pretty wood-frame home, and we had a healthy, adorable son bouncing in his Johnny Jump-Up in the kitchen. Then Larry showed up at our doorstep. I felt ill at the sight of him. He reeked of oil and smoke and leather. He was filthy and sullen, and—like a nasty animal—I didn't want him in the house, on my furniture. But Scott believed Larry was really harmless to others—he was too bent on destroying himself. And in spite of the fact that we lived next door to our church, Scott insisted we welcome Larry into our home. I wondered what sort of gossip might be flying with a druggie's motorcycle parked in our driveway. Scott's never been one to concern himself with gossip. He simply cares about people.

I'll never forget the look on Larry's face when he first saw our baby. It was like Zachary brought a brief glimmer of joy and light into Larry's cave-like existence. Larry would actually smile and soften and talk baby talk as Zach jumped up and down in his little seat, squealing with delight. I marveled at the contrast between the two of them and wondered what, in our baby's face, might be speaking to Larry. I kept a close and watchful eye.

One evening, Larry dropped by and I made him a simple supper. Then we all sat in the living room and Larry began to describe a nightmare he'd had the night before. It scared him so much that he wasn't able to get back to sleep and was afraid to go to sleep again. In his vivid dream he saw demons and evil and darkness and death. I could not hold my tongue.

"Larry," I said, "I really think God's trying to get your attention. Please, *wake up!* You've gotta get help. I know this may sound hokey, but I believe in the reality of evil forces, even satanic beings. You need to call out to Christ, Larry."

"Yeah," Larry slurred his thick words, "I believed in Jesus when I was a kid. Lot of good it did me."

"You know," Scott added gently, "you probably did trust in Jesus a long time ago. I remember that you once told me you had. But how you live your life is your responsibility. You make the choices. And your life is not only mocking God; it's killing everyone who loves you to watch you self-destruct."

Suddenly, the living room grew quiet.

"Larry," I said urgently as he started to get up, "I'm not playing around. I really think that dream means something important. For some reason I don't think you have much time left."

Larry moved to leave and said, "It scares the —————— out of me, but I think you're right."

Two days later, on a sunny Saturday afternoon, Larry dropped by again. He hadn't changed his clothes for at least a week. His face was covered with soot, the smell of smoke and oil filled the air.

"I'm really sick," Larry mumbled as he stumbled toward the living room. "I just need to lay down for a minute and rest before I drive the rest of the way home."

Scott nodded, got Larry a drink of water and a pillow, and let him rest on the couch. While Larry slept, I went back in the bedroom to nap with baby Zach, and Scott sat across from Larry in an easy chair working on some school papers. The house was quiet and serene—even in the back bedroom the stillness was palpable. Peace fell softly, like a warm down blanket around our home. Scott looked up from his papers at Larry resting and thought, *I think this is the only time I've ever looked at Larry and thought he looked at rest. I'll let him sleep as long as he wants.*

Several minutes later Scott looked up again and realized that Larry's chest was not moving. "Oh, God," Scott said quietly, moving to check Larry's pulse. There was none.

Two days later Scott and I stood arm in arm at the simple graveside service. Larry's mother, a woman of amazing strength and courage, cried silent tears. Larry had been her only son. Her heart was breaking, but then, her heart had been breaking for a long, long time. In a way, she was free—free from the torturous pain of watching her son walk a daily, living death. As we stood under the green canopy in front of Larry's casket, his mom encircled Scott with a hug and asked him to say a few words. Scott spoke of Larry's good qualities and of their friendship. Then he spoke of forks in the road, of significant choices, of human weakness and pain, and finally of eternal hope, and of God's mercy.

And so, with a sigh, I listen now as my children's father tells the story. The tale of two friends on two motorcycles and two roads that once diverged on a highway. Of a path that leads to life. And of another path—whose end is death. And he urges his children, as one who knows, to take the road less traveled by.

This is what the LORD says:
"Stand at the crossroads and look; . . .
ask where the good way is, and walk in it,
and you will find rest for your souls."
JEREMIAH 6:16

I'm Gonna Change the World!

B etween Scott's "wild" days and the time we would eventually fall in love, he and I became good "church buddies"—both of us oozing with idealism. Other kids our age were just *kids*. *We* were different; we were going to change the world. So when we read about an organization that sent teenagers out on summer work teams to make a real difference to needy people in foreign lands, we signed up right away. A prerequisite for getting to Central America (our chosen field) was to attend a week-long boot camp in the swamps of Florida.

And so in the summer of 1974, a sixteen-year-old boy and a fifteen-year-old girl ended up in an airport in Dallas saying teary good-byes to their families for the summer. They each held a squared-off shovel—donations for their work project. The thin, blond boy also held a box of stationery outlined with the map of the world; his mom hoped it would encourage him to write home. The girl—a cheerful brunette—busied herself with alternately losing and finding her purse. Oddly, the two teenagers seemed to share a penchant for running into walls and tripping on carpet. The mother of the girl turned to the mother of the boy, her eyes pleading.

"Is your son, by any chance, a 'together' sort of person? Because you see, actually . . . well . . . my daughter is *not*."

The mother of the son swallowed hard and shook her head. Both mothers gripped the guardrail a bit tighter as the silver plane took off with their offspring—their offspring who could not be trusted to keep up with their own shoes, much less their passports.

That was the summer the fifteen-year-old girl fell in love with the sixteen-year-old boy, and together they grew up to be me and Scott.

Two weeks ago, Scott and I found ourselves once again walking around in the Dallas–Fort Worth airport. Our teenage son, Ezekiel, walked in front of us, shovel in hand. That's when the airport began taking on the feel of a time-warp tunnel.

You see, our lanky blond son was heading to boot camp in Florida and then on to Guatemala with the same organization his father and I had gone with more than twenty years ago. Besides the shovel, Zeke was also carrying a box of stationery, faded and outlined with a map of the world—a gift from his grandmother, Scott's mom. I silently prayed it would encourage him to write home. Walking beside Zeke was a fifteen-year-old girl, Rachel Morris, heading toward the same destination. She's just a buddy. Brunette. Winsome smile. I soon found Rachel's mother, Deborah, and cornered her with a question.

"Look, Deb, is your daughter, by any chance, a 'together' sort of girl? Because to tell you the truth our Zeke . . . well . . . he's *not*."

Deborah shook her head. "Are you *kidding?* She's forever losing her purse. That's why I got her that little pack that attaches to her back."

Uh-oh.

An attendant asked the passengers to begin boarding, and I smiled bravely and walked with my son to the entrance ramp. But as soon as his back turned the corner, I ran to my husband's embrace and bawled like a baby. Elizabeth Stone once said, "Making the decision to have a child—it's momentous. It is to decide forever to have your heart go walking around outside your body."[7]

Had it been this hard for my own parents to tell me good-bye that summer of 1974? I only had to look over at them now—our parents, Zeke's grandparents—to see the answer to my question. Their eyes were pools about to overflow. Daddy stayed close by my side until his grandson's airplane disappeared from sight, offering a shoulder as I felt a big hunk of my heart take off with Zeke.

It was eerie and comforting, knowing my dad had been in my shoes. As a matter of fact, as we calculated the years, we figured out that Scott and I were the exact same age my parents had been when we had left for our trip. Funny. My parents had seemed so much more mature than we are.

On the way home I thought, *Seven weeks—seven whole weeks without my child! I will die, that's all, I will just die from this ache in my heart by the end of the summer.* Then I had a wild thought, and soon the wild thought took on a life of its own—shaping and twisting itself into a wild, full-blown plan. I broached the subject with Scott—carefully.

"Listen to my whole speech before you say no, OK? What if—now hear me out—what if we flew to Florida in a couple of weeks to see Zeke at his commissioning from boot camp? Before he leaves the country? I know it's expensive, but Visa would let us pay it all out, I'm sure about that. And we could see the old boot camp again.

"Remember how you led the obstacle course and were the big macho hero of our team? Remember how beautiful it was when all the kids lit candles on commissioning night? Remember the circus tent and the loud, wonderful songs we sang underneath it? The hopes, the prayers? Remember how we were so young and how we were going to change the world and how we ended up falling in love instead? But falling in love was pretty good, wasn't it? And maybe Zeke will change the world. Just in case he's about to do it, we should fly down to Florida to see him, don't you think?"

I drew a deep breath and waited. Scott shrugged his shoulders.

"OK," he said.

"OK?"

"Yep. OK."

And so we did.

Upon our arrival, our son walked out of the jungle like Tarzan. Or maybe more like Cheetah. Anyway, he was filthy and happy. I'd written him that we might be coming, but I think he was still surprised to see we'd really come.

"Hey, Dad!" he said, giving us both an enthusiastic, grubby hug, "I'm leading our team in the obstacle course! We are *taking* this camp, man!"

The gleam of pride in Scott's eye did not escape my notice. Our son gave us the grand tour of the camp while mosquitoes enjoyed a gourmet meal on freshly-flown-in flesh. After a camp-style supper, Zeke cleaned himself up and together we headed for the big top and the big night—the last night of boot camp.

Almost 2,000 kids gathered under the giant tent—in our day there were only about 400, as I recall. But the lively choruses they sang were the same, and as we sang, I was fifteen all over again. An African youth choir shuffled rhythmically down the aisles in their native costumes, singing to the beat of bongo drums.

"I'm gonna shake, shake, shake de world! I'm gonna shake de world for Jesus! I'm gonna shake, shake, shake de world! Gonna shake de world for Him!"

I remembered. I was, too. I was going to shake the world. Me and God. And Scott.

Bob Bland, the ordinary looking but amazing founder of Teen Missions, stood to speak. He hadn't changed at all, other than the silver in his hair. We'd seen him earlier—riding around the camp on a bicycle, wearing jeans, a T-shirt, and his famous wide smile. And, of course, he was barking orders as he sailed by.

Yet we knew he must be in his mid-sixties. Over the last twenty-five years Bob and his precious wife, Bernie, have given more than 30,000 teenagers the opportunity to serve and grow in other countries.

As Bob asked former team members to stand up and shout out the year and country they had visited, Scott and I obliged. In unison we yelled, "El Salvador! 1974!" It was soon apparent that we were both so—so *old*. No one else even came close to our decade.

Moving toward the final ceremony, the floodlights were turned off, and blackness settled over the tent. Reverently, Bob Bland recited one of my favorite quotes, "It is better to light one candle than to shout at the darkness." With that he lit his candle and others followed one by one, as the teens accepted the challenge to be lights in their world. Our loving, giving, incredible son was among them. Just yesterday, it seems, we were too.

That night we said good-bye to Zeke for the second time in two weeks, and my heart tore once again. This time he would be flying toward a land of volcanoes, lush foliage, and gentle Mayans. He would be helping to construct a building and working with handicapped Guatemalans—wonderfully and terribly exciting.

I remember how it felt. I was there, Zeke. I was fifteen once. Only I am a mother now, and along with the excitement and joy, I will worry about your safety and I will ache every night missing you. It's what mothers do, and it seems nobody can help that.

But I will let you go, and I will pray for you, because I have no other choice. You are our child, and what beats inside our hearts now beats inside yours. Go forth and make a difference. Shake the world upside down, our son.

Your life is already shaking ours. All over again.

Back home we soon got a letter from Zeke. It read,

Mom and Dad,

I guess you should know me and Rachel have fallen madly in love and that we hope to be just like y'all and marry as soon as we arrive.

Love all y'all!
Zeke

He's quite a little kidder, that boy. (You *do* think he's kidding, don't you?)

> *Even youths grow tired and weary . . . but . . .*
> *the LORD will renew their strength.*
> *They will soar on wings like eagles.*
> ISAIAH 40:30–31

ぇ

FIFTEEN

Hey, Mom!
I've Got a Job!

A couple of springs ago, some good friends of ours, Karl and Terry Kemp, sent us a graduation announcement in honor of their son, Joshua. Inside was a dashing picture of Josh, age seventeen and wearing a tuxedo.

The fancy script engraving on the card read as follows:

Whereas
Joshua Adam Kemp
has completed the course of study required of him
pursuant to achieving mastery of matters academic; and
Whereas
he has a job, pays for his car insurance,
pumps his own gas and eats out
when he jolly well pleases; and
Whereas
He is able to converse at the dinner table with wit and
erudition

without even mentioning boogers,
Let it be known henceforth
to all peoples that
he is a big boy now.

I reread the card several times, laughing out loud.

Joshua was the first baby born to our circle of college friends. It wasn't long before the rest of us followed suit and began having babies of our own. This baby-birthing period was sort of like a popcorn machine: First, one baby kernel popped. Then after a while, another burst forth. Then all of a sudden it was poppoppoppoppop—and soon there was popcorn (or, in this case, babies) everywhere we looked. Then, eventually, it all slowed down. Pop-pop. Pop. Pop. Pop. We looked up one day and, suddenly, none of us were popping out babies anymore. We were having teenagers instead.

Which brings us to the present. When I realized that Joshua was a full-fledged teenager on the verge of graduating and leaving home and all the things that go with these emotional rites of passage, I knew our turn to watch our own kids take flight was up next. Josh simply blew the whistle of "things to come." It won't be long before my oldest son, Zachary, is officially a big boy too—heading out the family door to the waiting world.

Zachary just turned sixteen. The number's still pretty new to me. I'm having a little difficulty even putting it down on paper, since he's only been carrying this age around for a month. The age of sixteen, as you know, traditionally ushers in a new driver and, hopefully, a job. Zachary just began pumping gas at a local convenience store. Bless Zach's heart, when it comes to learning a new job the transition from childhood to adulthood is more than just a rite of passage; sometimes it's more like a riot of passage. As a matter of fact, Zach's boss just called last week to warn us that our son would be coming home early, and then added, "Now don't be too shocked when you first see him. It's not as bad as it looks."

As Scott and I sat on the back porch puzzling over what this might mean, our teenager rounded the bend and our mouths simultaneously dropped open. Zach was literally covered from head to foot with great globs of dripping black grease. He looked like a toxic waste accident in Nike tennis shoes. Scott handed him a bucket of grease remover, and after he'd cleaned up the worst of it, the story unfolded.

Seems a customer had pulled up to the station and asked Zach to put a couple of quarts of oil in his car. Zach cheerfully agreed to the task. When the man came out of the store and saw what Zachary was doing (which was in truth, simply following orders) the man yelled, "Son, you didn't put all of the two quarts of oil in there did you?"

Puzzled by the man's rage, Zach answered, "Yes sir, I did."

"Well," ranted the irate customer, "you've got to get under there and take out the plug and let some of it out right now. You overfilled it."

Zach, being young and still of a mind to try to please the man, obliged. It might have worked, had the plug not broken loose while Zach was twisting it off the bottom of the oil pan. (Zachary would like me to point out, in his defense, that the plug coming loose is a common occurrence in these situations.) As things were, Zach ended up on the receiving end of an oil bath. Only a few weeks earlier, Zach had accidentally poured a quart of oil in a customer's radiator. Needless to say, he was pretty discouraged.

I identified with Zach's troubles because I also had a miserable time adjusting to new jobs as a teenager. Actually, come to think of it, Zach's already much farther along than I was at his age.

The first job I ever held was a summer baby-sitting job for a family with a brand-new home. I was fifteen. Wanting to impress them by baking a hot apple pie, I opened the preheated oven door (which was so new it still had a sticker on it) and a hot skillet slipped out. Then it fell with a sickening sizzle-thud onto the freshly laid floor. When I pulled the skillet up, a big gooey circle of melted vinyl came up with it. Crying profusely, I telephoned the father to prepare him for the decorating adjustment I'd just made to his two-week-old home. I could barely talk between sobs, and by the time I finally got the story out, the poor father was simply overtaken with joy that no one had died.

Eventually I graduated from baby-sitting to a secretarial position at a health club. One day my boss called me into his office, and I was certain he was going to offer me a raise. After all, I was "friendly" personified. Instead he said, "Becky, you are a nice receptionist, with a lovely phone voice and all—but I can't have an employee who consistently hangs up the receiver on my clientele three to four times an afternoon. Giggling 'Ooops, I'm so sorry, I did it again' just isn't cutting it anymore. I'm afraid we're going to have to let you go." I couldn't believe it. I'd been fired! And me, such a nice girl.

Then there was my short stint as a pharmacist's assistant. (I know what you are thinking. Now there's a scary thought: a teenage girl who can't handle phone buttons dispensing prescription drugs.) I'll never forget the time a customer walked up to the counter and asked for Neosporin. I thought he said his name was Neil Sporin, so I came back with, "I'm sorry. I can't find it. How do you spell that last name again?" On another occasion, the pharmacist caught me typing up instructions for a patient to "Take one suppository, two times a day, by mouth." At that point, he and I both came to the conclusion that my talents might be better placed elsewhere. Far, far elsewhere.

And so, when I received yet another call from Zach's boss this morning, I was more sympathetic than the average mother might have been. Thankfully, she was laughing this time. "Becky," she said, "you haven't finished Zach's chapter have you? Because I've got another good one for you."

"No," I answered, grabbing for a pen and paper. "What do you have on him now?"

"Well," she answered, "Zach accidentally left his application for a D-FY-IT card here at the store. (A D-FY-IT card is a discount card the teenagers in our school district can receive if they pass a drug test and promise to stay drug-free.) The questionnaire asked for the students to describe any prescriptions or over-the-counter pharmaceutical products they may have taken in the last twenty-four hours. Zachary, wanting so badly to be conscientious, made sure he'd covered all the bases. His drug list? Aspirin, Crest, Speed Stick deodorant, and Barbisol shaving cream. (I can see some police officer chuckling, "Son, when was the last time you got high on toothpaste?" or even better, "I'm sorry, Mr. Freeman, but I'm going to have to book you for possession of deodorant.")

As time passes I'm sure Zachary (and his mom) will survive all the rites, and the riots, of teenage passage. He's well on his way to becoming a big boy. Mistakes, unfortunately, are a necessary part of the journey. All of us had to learn our share of lessons from them.

It seems to encourage Zach, somewhat, to know that even his mother, once a scatterbrained teenage girl, arrived safely to scatterbrained adulthood. Of course, I never did succeed at holding down a regular, steady job. I'm still in the embarrassing position of having to explain, "Yes, I have a degree in elementary education and taught first grade. But I'm a retired teacher now—after nine long months of faithful service." There is a happy ending to my job search, however. I finally figured out a way to make a modest living—writing about the very messes I've been accumulating all my life. ("See, Mom and Dad, there was nothing to worry about all along.")

George MacDonald wrote, "When we are out of sympathy with the young, our work in this world is over." Well, George, looks like I can relax. Because with all the sympathy I have for teenagers, I'm going to have steady work in this world for a very long time.

Being confident of this, that he who began a
good work in you will carry it on to completion.

PHILIPPIANS 1:6

&

I Don't Wanna Go to Church Anymore!

"What is it? What's wrong with me?"

I set my cup down on the coffee shop table as I rested the side of my face on the palm of my hand. As long as I was in this far, I went ahead and unleashed the rest of it. "I can't stand church."

It was a childish statement—exaggerated, to be sure—but it welled up within me in a candid, unguarded moment and spilled out into the atmosphere. And there my confession hung for a few seconds, suspended, like a soap bubble before it bursts. My three girlfriends blinked in unison around the table and took deep consecutive breaths before diving into the interrogation.

"What's there not to like, Becky? Is it the color of the carpet? the song selections?"

"I don't know," I fumbled. "Yes. No. I don't know!"

"Is it the people? Are they not friendly?"

"Yes. No. Oh, I don't know!"

"Are you OK with your relationship with God?"

"Yes—oh, *yes!* It's wonderful—He's wonderful. I'm more assured of God's love than I've ever been. I'm especially enjoying reading slowly through the Gospels, but I'm finding more and more that I want to read them *alone*—not be involved in a study group. I have you guys and other Christian friends I love to be with—you know that. We lunch, we pray, we share each other's lives. I come away filled and renewed. But for some reason, lately I'm wanting to hibernate from church. I come away empty and relieved that the ordeal is over. What is wrong with me?" We talked around the subject for nearly an hour.

This morning, I sit alone, sipping my coffee and staring out the window at the overcast coolness of the morning. I mull over my unenthusiastic feelings about going to church. I find, surprisingly, there are stirrings inside me similar to those of an angry little girl. The grown-up part of my head argues back with plenty of "shoulds" and "oughts"—like that Frosted Mini Wheats commercial where the "adult" on the outside battles emotions with the outspoken "kid" inside.

But this time, the childish feelings prevail—strongly. I read two things that made me feel a little better. One is from Paula Hardin's book, *What Are You Doing with the Rest of Your Life?* "In middle adulthood," she writes, "the inner child long denied becomes increasingly insistent. It wants to be heard."[8] Now, I've not completely bought into this "inner child" stuff—much of it smacks of New Agey egocentric mumbo. But something in my soul warns, *Don't throw out the inner child with the New Age bathtub. For inside everyone there is a child who needs to be loved and accepted. We are, eternally, children to our Heavenly Father. Not only is this concept biblical, it is a childlike part of us we can never outgrow. Nor should we want to.*

Second, something a young boy said in Sunday school brings the corners of my mouth up in a weak smile. "When Jesus was my age, He went to church with a bunch of people and got lost. It happens."[9] I think Jesus understands what is happening to me. I'm probably one of thousands who've felt lost in church. It happens.

Still, I'm alarmed to find I am close to tears. What if I were ten years old, headstrong, honest, and outspoken—what would I be bursting to say right now? Imagine . . . if I were to take Jesus at His words this morning and come to Him as a child, what would I say to Him? How would I express my feelings about church, about Him? How would it all come tumbling out? I might ramble. I might say things I shouldn't. If I were a child, sitting on the grass having a conversation with Jesus, what would I say? Perhaps I'd start with something like . . .

Jesus, I love You—but can we talk about this "church thing" for a minute? First of all, I do not understand why I'm supposed to dress up fancy to come to church. Why do I have to wear dresses that itch and shoes that hurt, and curl my hair to come visit Your house? Who made up Sunday school clothes? If you meant what You said—if You want people to come to You as a child—how come everybody doesn't just wear overalls and T-shirts and Keds and ponytails and baseball caps, or even feety pajamas, to church? and maybe even run through a mud puddle on the way in the door? I'd like to wring the neck of the person who came up with the big idea that we should all look la-di-da-dressy for church.

Another thing. In the Bible, You got to have church *outside.* Oh, You visited fancy temples now and then, but maybe just to keep Your foot in the door. When it was up to You, You had church out under the sky by a lake or on a grassy hill or in a boat. You didn't need fancy banners or stained-glass windows—Your sun painted the background with bursty oranges and purples and reds. You didn't need an organist playing worshipy mood music—Your Sea of Galilee made pretty, smooth sounds with its waves dropping onto the shore. And Your birds sang from the trees in between Your words. I wish I could have gone to Your outside church.

There's another thing I don't like about church: the sermons. I especially don't like the little outlines with every point starting with the same letter of the alphabet. Who teaches this stuff to preachers anyway? I don't want to hear about The Position, The

Principles, and The Promise anymore. (And is there really even supposed to be just one "big teacher"?)

What I really want to know is what happened to my brothers and sisters this week. Where were they when they met with God? What words did He say to their hearts? And did they laugh, did they cry, did they sing or dance with the joy of it? I also want to hear stories. Short ones. Like the ones You told, Jesus. Children like little stories a whole lot. I'll tell You another secret: I think their parents do too.

And by the way, in every church there should be lots of nice old people—the kind whose skin has gotten too big for them, so it kind of hangs wiggly under their chins. The kind who are especially nice to children. It's especially good if they keep gum or candy in their pockets to hand out after church, if moms and dads will let their kids have some. (And their moms and dads should let them have some.) I wonder, did You carry treats around in Your robe pocket, just in case? It probably didn't matter if You did or not. The kids all loved You anyway, because You were kind and noticed them.

By the way—do You know what my favorite miracle is? It was the time that all those gobs of people were listening to You, and they loved Your stories so much they forgot to stop and eat. Remember that time? And remember how those grown-up disciples of Yours were all worried and stressed out because there wasn't any food? I think it is funny that You had to find Yourself a calm, quiet little boy to help You out. Sometimes grown-ups just get in the way. I would love to have seen the big people's faces when that boy's lunch just kept growing and growing and growing. I wonder if somebody put up golden arches later that said, "Over 5,000 served from five loaves and two fishes." I wish I could have been the kid with the lunch that day.

This is kinda off the subject, but I'd just like to mention that I think food's a good thing to have around at church. I've always liked church suppers—where everybody brings something to share with everybody else. Especially the coconut cake and the

Mexican salad. I get really, really thankful for lunch when there is coconut cake and Mexican salad.

OK, back to the part I hate most about church, if You want to know the truth. Church reminds me too much of school. It's too big, there are too many people, there's too much sitting and listening. I'm not good at trying to squeeze into talking groups of people or wandering around in halls hoping I look like I know what I'm doing. I think certain grown-ups feel really bad admitting they don't like to go to church a whole lot, because they are supposed to love being around people so much. But the truth of the matter is, even grown-ups sometimes feel lost and alone in the middle of crowds—and would like to just go get donuts and go home.

Sometimes, I wonder how people who aren't born and raised in church ever get the gumption to go visit the first time. And lots of them *actually come back again.* I think probably it is the real strong talkers and good dressers that get most gung ho about it all.

Why couldn't we just skip Big Church? And then everybody who loves You could just get together at the donut shop. And they could tell each other where they met God last week, what His words sounded like to them, and whether the words made them laugh or cry or sing or dance. Share stories, You know. Then they could pray, sing a song, and go home. If church were like this, I might even could do it every other day.

"Oh, grow up," I can hear someone out there saying. Well, I have just one thing to say to that someone: I think you are mean and ugly, and I don't like your shirt.

Tell you what, I think I need a time out or a nap or some juice and cookies. Can we pick this subject up in the next chapter when I'm not feeling quite so sleepy and grumpy?

> *He went back to teaching by the sea. . . .*
> *He taught by using stories, many stories.*
> MARK 4:1, THE MESSAGE

Jesus Is Easier to Love Than His Kids

All right, all right. I've had my cookie break and nappy time. I'm feeling more mature, and the child in me has had her big say. I'm teasing about it, but truthfully it is a big relief to get those pent-up childish "whines" out of my system.

Alas, however, the grown-up left in charge of my mind is wondering, *What now?* The solution is not to change churches. All of them, every single one of them, has its own set of problems. People tend to be very candid with me, so this much I do know: I am not alone in my frustration. Church rejects, outcasts, and misfits are everywhere and are immensely relieved to find a sympathetic ear. In my humble opinion, we should listen to them every once in a while, that is, if the church truly wants to understand and love people.

One of the most obvious problems in all denominations is that church people are capable of inflicting so much pain on one another.

This week, I visited with two other precious women who have burgeoning ministries in writing and speaking. We each shared our own "horror stories"—the occasional nasty letter or rude verbal rejection they receive from, of course, well-meaning church ladies. We all admitted we sometimes struggle with the pain of these comments even months and years later. Though it was strangely therapeutic to know our experiences were not isolated cases, it saddened me to realize the sort of grief the church is capable of imparting to its own.

I also had an interesting conversation with a complete stranger in a public rest room a few months ago. I had just picked up a dress from the dry cleaners, and since I had to hurry on to a speaking event, I decided to change into the dress while in the rest room of a local grocery store.

As I was digging into my makeup bag, a woman walked in, observed my dolling up, and commented, "Nice dress. You going to church?"

"No," I answered, "but I'm about to go somewhere and give a little talk, and I'll probably say some good things about God. Does that count?"

She laughed a little and said, "You know, I'd like to believe in a good God." Then quickly she confessed, "I used to go to church every Sunday. But I was so hurt by some of the people there, I've never gone back again."

I turned toward her as I finished tightening the back of an earring and gently, *carefully* said, "Did you ever read that story in the Bible where the mothers took their children to Jesus to be blessed? I always thought it was kind of ironic that it was the disciples, Jesus' followers, who almost kept those kids from running into Jesus' arms."

"I never thought about it that way, but it's true. And it's *His people* that make me want to avoid everything having to do with Jesus and His church."

"Just remember, Jesus is really, really different than many of His followers act. They often mean well. But lots of us still don't know what we are doing, and the church has a lot of growing to do. Please don't let Christians stop you from running to Him like a kid needing a hug. He loves you so much."

She smiled, and as she turned to leave, she said, "Thanks, I needed to hear that."

I wondered, *Is it possible this woman found more compassion in our over-the-sink encounter than she'd been able to find from her years in an organized church?* The thought frustrated and then angered me. It is so easy to understand why so many people do not feel that the benefits of belonging to church are worth the pain involved. And many feel that if they left, they wouldn't be missed—like taking a teaspoon of sand from the desert. "The professionals are in charge anyway. Who needs me?"

I know a wonderful, God-fearing woman who grew up in a wonderful, God-loving, church-going home. She also adored her father, who pastored one of the most well-known churches in America. Today she's married to a wonderful, God-loving, church-going man. However, the "church-going" part is something she no longer feels an obligation to do. I also know a terrific marriage counselor, a deeply spiritual, compassionate man. God's love pours through him as he comforts hurting people in his office every day. But he's also said, "Thank you, but no thank you" to much involvement in a regular, formal church. Been there, done that, got burned, gonna avoid it.

I have to admit there's something about their decisions I admire. I think sometimes I, too, shall simply cross church off my "to do" list and be done with it. And yet . . .

What would happen if the traditional, organized church disappeared from the American scene? I must confess, I'd be devastated. It would be a terrible loss for our country. I think of my friends, Igor and Elaine, who grew up in the days of a "godless, churchless" Russia. (This was, what? A handful of years ago?) To attend an organized, underground worship service might, at any time, turn into a life-threatening event. Elaine's father, the pastor, was dragged away to prison twice for his faith. There was only one Bible in their church, and it had to be passed around in secret from family to family. When Elaine's family got their turn at the Bible it was like Christmas and New Year's all rolled into one.

I think, sometimes, I am spoiled, not remembering what a privilege it is to assemble en masse, openly, to worship. My husband hastens to remind me that one of the main purposes in coming together in a "Big Church" setting is to honor God and worship Him as a whole; it is not simply about getting *our* human needs met. *Oh, yeah,* whispers the little girl in me, *I forgetted that part.*

Also, I must admit, with all its faults, the structure of a formal church gives our children healthy places to go and sweet, decent kids with whom to hang out. Because of the youth group, my oldest boys have had opportunities to minister to orphans and the poorest of the poor on summer mission trips. I met my own husband, twenty years ago, in a church youth group. Come to think of it, I've met most of my best, lifelong friends in some pocket of a church setting. Even the women to whom I made my horrible I-don't-like-church confession are friends I made—you guessed it—at church.

There is no easy answer to the complexities in the Christian church today. The bad news is: Church is imperfect; it does not meet everyone's needs; it sometimes does more harm than it does good. I don't even know why they call it the "organized church" because it usually appears anything but organized with its members fussing and fighting and pulling and pushing—often on front pages of newspapers for all the world to see and cluck their tongues at. Let's face it: Sometimes it's plain embarrassing to admit holding membership in this God-ordained family of feuders.

The good news is: Since the church is imperfect, it won't shake things up much if the likes of you and I join in. Often, too, there are moments of glory when the church responds from its heart and does a great deal of good. Mother Teresa and her tender work among lepers is sanctioned and funded by a church. (Maybe not your particular denomination, but still, part of the Church Universal.) During the Nazi reign, Corrie ten Boom and members of her church risked and gave their lives to save Jewish families and friends.

Ironically, my hometown of Greenville is suddenly being blasted across national headlines and "honored" with visits from the New Black Panthers and the Ku Klux Klan. (I've yet to hear of one citizen, black or white, who welcomes either group here.) I stood in a stadium Sunday night, looking out over a salt-and-pepper sea of thousands of black and white Christians praying together as Dr. Tony Evans led us in a call to unity and peace. There were very few dry eyes as the crowd joined hands singing, "Bind us together, Lord." It is in these shining moments that I know that this mystery called "the body of Christ" has all the potential of being the eyes, hands, and compassion of Jesus to a confused and angry world. If only church happened like this every Sunday. If only it did not take an enemy's assault to "bind us together with love."

Last night I came across a well-worn book, authored by Philip Yancey. Actually, I didn't know it was a book—at first I thought it was a lump. I felt something stuck down the side of my mattress and, curious as to the origin of the lump, I fished around and pulled it out and discovered it was, after all, Yancey's book. (Whole libraries of used books and drawers full of socks and bags full of cookie crumbs live between the mattresses and under my bed. We could sustain our family for months from the haphazard rations pushed, swept, shoved, and stored there.)

Anyway, I've become a huge Philip Yancey fan since having heard him speak and having read his books. I am so grateful for this thoughtful, honest, intelligent, fuzzy-haired brother in Christ. He has a way of putting so much that is puzzling—about the Christian life, about God, about pain, about the Bible—into meaningful chunks I can slowly, methodically digest. I just finished his latest book, *The Jesus I Never Knew,* and believe it is perhaps the most significant book I've ever read. But the worn-out Yancey book under my bed happened to be one of his earlier classics, *Disappointment with God.*[10]

I try not to quote extensively from the writings of others. This practice is often a tactic for writers too lazy to fill empty pages with their own thoughts. (I think my mother told me this; it sounds like one of her Momilies.) However, I'm going to make a small exception. For those among us who admit to episodes of being disappointed, not only with God, but also with church, I do not think I can possibly offer more wisdom and insight than Yancey's observations on this subject. To begin with, he raises a series of rhetorical questions that I could easily "Amen."

> The manifold wisdom of God being made known through the church? Have you been to church lately? Jesus would have been impressive; the shekinah glory cloud would have stopped you flat; but the church?

Yes, Philip, I am as stumped as you are. Maybe the problem is that our modern westernized American services have strayed from the original guidelines of the early church. Mr. Yancey gently, but firmly, protests that argument.

> I cannot agree. The Epistles were written to a motley crew of converted angel worshipers, thieves, idolaters, backbiters, and prostitutes—those were the people in whom God took up residence. Read Paul's descriptions of the supposed "ideal church" in a city like Corinth: a raucous, ornery bunch that rivals any church in history for their unholiness. And yet Paul's most stirring depiction of the church as Christ's body appears in a letter to them.

But look what a mess the church has left in its wake throughout history! On this point, at least, Yancey agrees.

> The church's obvious defects would seem to be the greatest cost to God. Just as He committed His name to the nation Israel and had it dragged through mud, He now commits His Spirit to flawed human beings. You don't have to look far—the church in Corinth, racism in South Africa, bloodshed in Northern Ireland, scandals among U.S. Christians—for proof that the church does not measure up to God's ideal. And the watching world judges God by those who carry his name. A large measure of disappointment with God stems from disillusionment with other Christians.

That's exactly what I have been saying! Have you been reading my mind? Then why, for God's own sake, is He allowing holier-than-thous, nitpickers, wimps, odd birds, etc., to go on making an embarrassing wreck of things, misrepresenting His nature? Surely there's a better way. Yancey explains that God's way rarely follows earthly logic in His passionate pursuit of reconciliation with humankind.

> Dorothy Sayers has said that God underwent three great humiliations in His efforts to rescue the human race. The first was the Incarnation, when He took on the confines of a physical body. The second was the Cross, when He suffered the ignominy of public execution. The third humiliation, Sayers suggested, is the Church. In an awesome act of self-denial, God entrusted His reputation to ordinary people.

Oh.

So, let me get this straight: God Almighty is trusting ordinary quirky people like me? Whiners like me? A woman/child like me? To represent the love and compassion of Christ? Wow. The little girl in me raises her tiny wavering voice to say, I think maybe God should know I'm not big enough for this important of a job.

It dawns on me, astonishes me, as I realize we humans not only place our faith in God; He has also chosen to place His faith in *us*, His church.

OK, Lord, then show me what it is You see through my human eyes. What is it You want to say through my faltering voice—this peculiar Texas accent of mine? Where do You want me to go? To church? To bathrooms of grocery stores? You show me, I'll go.

I can't believe this. As I'm writing, the phone rings. It is a woman from my church wanting to know if I'd emcee the Ladies' Camp Retreat this year. How about that? I haven't been completely written off as potential church material in spite of my less-than-stellar attendance.

So, Lord. Are You saying You want me to go to camp? OK, I can deal with this. I like camp. I can wear sweatpants and feety pajamas and eat donuts there. Unlike formal church, everyone's not in a big hurry to rush off to the next service. I can take time to get to know a few ladies, one at a time, at my own snail's pace.

I say to the woman on the phone, "Yes, I'm honored to be asked."

Next day. Still editing, finalizing this chapter. The phone rings again. "Becky?" I recognize the voice immediately. It is another friend from church whom I've not seen for a couple of months. I remember now that I miss this friend's voice. She and I have prayed each other through valleys of tears. She also makes me laugh with a funny story about her daughter's latest antics. Then she gets right to the point. "Becky, I've been elected to call you because I'm the only one on our committee who's not afraid to ask you to speak at our October women's event. Here's the catch—we have no money for a speaking budget. It would have to be a freebie."

I laugh. Offend me? Little does my friend know that it is the *committee ladies* who are encouraging *me* with this invitation. I'd never consider taking a fee for speaking at my home church. Oh, now listen to me. My *home church.* Just a wee bit of encouragement and I'm already making noises like a church lady again. Perhaps, the greatest need in the body of Christ is very simple. All of us—in some way—desperately need to feel that we are needed, that we *belong,* and that we are at *home.*

Lord, just promise me one thing. If I ever start giving high-sounding speeches with three little points that all start with the same letter or start dressing in sensible shoes and button-up flowery dresses with lace collars—instruct a brave, honest little kid to come up to me, pull on my knee-highs, and say, "Lady, you wanna go for a walk outside? The sun is real pretty right now."

Then I'll also know it's time to kick off my shoes, put on my overalls, go for a walk outside in the grass or mud, and watch a sunset filled with bursty oranges and purples and reds. Time for a heart-to-heart talk, little girl to loving Father. Time to gain a bit of childlike perspective again.

Lord, teach us—Your Body, Your Church—
for Your Sake and the Sake of a Hurting World
to mature, to grow up . . .
into Children again.

All the believers . . . broke bread
in their homes and ate together with glad
and sincere hearts, praising God and enjoying
the favor of all the people.
And the Lord added to their number daily.
ACTS 2:44, 46–47
❧

I Do It Myself!

The French writer Collete hit the proverbial nail on the head when she wrote in *Earthly Paradise,* "There are days when solitude is a heady wine that intoxicates you with freedom."[11] One of the things I most looked forward to, as a child, about someday getting to Grown-up Land was that I knew I'd finally get to do stuff *all by myself.*

This old daydream of mine is leading up to a small confession: I'm feeding a childish indulgence on a regular basis—acting out, I suppose, the desire to prove I can do whatever I want to do, whenever I want to do it, and do it all by myself, thank you very much. At least, in one small area of my life. I have to admit that nearly every day of my adult life I stop by a convenience store to buy myself a little "treat"—a Coke, a Reese's candy bar, a stick of beef jerky, a box of Junior Mints, or some such delicacy. Or if I'm on a diet (which averages about every third day), I'll buy bottled water or a cup of coffee and simply sniff or gaze longingly in the direction of the candy bar aisle. Most often I wind up purchasing nonsensical fluff, completely void of nutritional, educational, or spiritual value. Though it is thoroughly politically and nutritionally incorrect, I'll confess: I adore these goody-seeking jaunts. I look forward to them as much as a nap in a hammock or thirty minutes alone with a good book.

I know, I know. It's probably a power issue fraught with a myriad of dangerous physiological, not to mention, psychological implications. Yet from earliest childhood, I've dreamed of the day I could be on my own, driving my own car, carrying my own coins, and buying my own treats sans the hassle of begging or pleading or finagling my parents. I'd fantasize of marching headlong into the corner store any old time I pleased, relishing the control I could wield over my own destiny. Would it be a soft drink, a snack cake, a candy bar, or a pickle today? *When I get to be a grown-up,* I'd think with abandoned glee, *why, I can go to the store all by myself! Without asking a single adult for permission or loose change!*

I must say, this is one of my few childhood fantasies that has actually panned out to my expectations. Of course, my requirements for what qualifies as excitement are admittedly low, but every day I so look forward to declaring this tiny bit of independence. Yep, a real rabble-rouser, that's me.

And if I have my druthers, I prefer the local out-in-the-sticks convenience stores—Big Daddy's, The Village Bait & Tackle Store, Get-It-Kwik. Sure, they are filled with the aroma of stale smoke and their offerings often consist of petrified edibles and RC Colas with aluminum lids doubling as dust catchers, but I get a kick out of these hometown mom-and-pop operations.

Why? Because I can walk into any one of these places with my baggy purple shorts, my old red "Go Lone Oak Buffalos" T-shirt, my hair pulled up with those squeegee contraptions, bare feet, no makeup, and of this I can rest assured: There will be someone in the store who looks even worse than me. All in all, I believe this ritual to be a relatively harmless addiction.

It is extremely important, of course, that I get away for my excursion—*all by myself.* I'm sneaky when the kids are home and it's time to head out, solo, for my treat fix. I've even been known to put the car in neutral and let it slide backward out of the driveway so as not to alert the troops I'm about to escape for a few moments' respite. Otherwise they start running out of the house like orphaned children stranded on a desert island, begging—as if for their life—to "go with." I used to relent and take them, but after umpteen fights over "he gots more stuff than me" and twenty dollars down the drain trying to even it all out, I realized one day I was *not* having fun anymore. So these days, I make my getaway quickly and quietly.

Besides, I sooth my conscience, *my kids will have to wait their own turns to be grown-ups and buy junk food whenever they want. I had to wait all my childhood for this coveted reward.*

Now that my oldest child, Zach, has been driving for nearly a month, I'm enjoying watching him discover the joy and privileges of semi-adulthood. It's been surprising to discover how beneficial it is to have an extra driver around the house. Zach no longer begs and prods me to take him from point A to points B through Z and back again. He can get there in his own car now *all by himself.* Not only does he take care of his own transportation, but also his snacks, his entertainment, and—more and more—his general all-over life, *all by himself.* Which means I get more luxurious time to spend *all by myself.*

My mother phoned the other day. She has a new car phone, and I can always tell when she is using it because she's convinced she must shout in order to be heard way out there on the highway—seeing as the cellular phone's so far from her telephone lines and all. She cannot believe the small receiver actually works—looks too much like a dime store toy, she says.

Anyway, via the cellular airwaves, I could hear Mother's hollering loud and clear. "SO SISTER, HOW ARE YOU HANDLING YOUR OLDEST SON DRIVING A CAR?" (Mother always calls me "Sister" whenever she talks to me via telephone. I have no idea why. I think it's a generic name system, a holdover from her West Texas roots where everyone coming in and out of the house was a sister or brother to somebody.)

"Mother," I answered in a voice I knew bordered on that of a preschool teacher's, "let's try to talk just a little more softly, please. I promise, that toy phone of yours works really well. But back to your question—I am *thrilled* that Zach's driving. This is one time in my life when my forgetful nature has been a real boon. I keep forgetting when Zach is gone, when he is supposed to be home, and what time I'm supposed to start worrying. The other night, I didn't even know he'd gone out—and I was taken completely off guard when Zach walked in the front door and apologized all over himself for being an hour late. Because I didn't want him to think I'm not a conscientious mother, I scolded, 'Son, you had me worried sick! What's the matter? You didn't have a quarter to call home?' Of course, I really should have added, 'Next time pick up the phone and let me know when you aren't in your bedroom!'"

Mother laughs so loud I think my eardrum will burst. "WELL, HONEY, THIS MAY BE A BIG LOAD OFF YOUR SHOULDERS, TO HAVE ZACH WITH WHEELS AND ALL!"

"Mother, I love you. But if you don't tone down that volume I'm going to have to put the phone down on the floor."

"Oops. I forgot. I just can't believe—"

"—that little toy phone works so well. I know. But trust me, it does. Now back to Zach again. My life has simplified overnight since Zachary got his own car. You know how he's always been chomping at the bit to do his own thing; and with his new freedom, our relationship has really relaxed and improved. I only wish I'd thought about getting him a driver's license when he was two!"

Our conversation wound down, but I can't say the same for the volume. After yelling good-bye (if you can't beat 'em, join 'em), I hung up from my conversation with Mother, massaging my right ear as I walked from the bedroom to the kitchen. Then I began pondering the all-by-myself experiences that mark our children's lives as they move from childhood into adulthood.

One day a newborn arrives into our arms. So helpless, needy. In the space of a few months, however, our baby is holding a bottle or cup—all by himself. The next thing we parents know, our once-helpless infant is crawling, toddling, breaking eggs, and pouring milk into cracks in the floor—all by himself. Then comes the tearful day our pint-sized children insist on walking into a brick building and down the hall into a school classroom—all by themselves—where some teacher forever takes over our position as Primary Daytime Adult Companion.

Other "solo" rites of passage come so quickly the rest of childhood flies by in a blur. They learn to ride a bike—alone. There's the milestone of watching our children insist they go can into the doctor's examining room—unattended by Mom. Next, they're driving a car by themselves. Out on dates, without a chaperone. Then, hopefully, they'll find and hold down a job— all by themselves. All by themselves, one day, our kids will choose a mate, set up housekeeping, and begin having babies of their own—babies that, in the span of a few short months, will be holding their own bottles, all by themselves. And the cycle will repeat itself all over again.

This process, though poignant, does not make me sad. It is a good thing to grow up comfortably with all our scheduled "premier solos," and to learn to be content in our moments alone. While working on my degree in early childhood education a few years back, I was asked to write and illustrate a children's book for a class assignment. I read my little book to classroom after classroom of children; they loved it, identified with it, and begged me to read it "just one more time." Without benefit of my lovely homemade fingerpainted illustrations, I will attempt to describe the pertinent scenes as I share the text. The title of my book was—appropriate to the topic at hand—*All By Myself.*

All By Myself

Sometimes when I am happy
and want to sing and dance

I'll find a place
A quiet place
To hide
All By Myself

I sing, I twirl
I put on a show
Where no one else
But me, will know

[scene of a tree house, little girl dancing and kicking up her heels]

Sometimes when I'm upset
and want to cry or scream

I'll find a place
A quiet place
To hide
All By Myself

I'll fuss, I'll stomp
I'll SHOUT, SHOUT, SHOUT!
Until The Mad is all yelled out.

[scene by trees and pond, little girl having a royal fit]

Sometimes when I feel crowded
and want to get away

[little girl surrounded and squished by numerous siblings]

I'll find a place
A quiet place
To hide
All By Myself

[little girl in bathtub, pink bubbles everywhere]

I hop in the tub
and scoot down low
And pop the bubbles
With my toe

Sometimes when I am tired
and want to fall asleep
[she's yawning]

———

I'll find a place
A quiet place
To hide
All By Myself

Then snuggle deep
inside my bed
My pillow sinks
beneath my head

[scene of pigtailed little girl, sitting on a window seat,
contentedly looking out at the world]

I like Myself
I'm nice to know
So with Myself
I like to go

Sometimes you see
I like to be
All by Myself
With only Me

© Becky Freeman

Funny. These all-by-my-lonesome ponderings have caused
me to work up an appetite. Perhaps I should get up and move
around a bit. Or better yet, run to the corner store and get an
ice-cold RC Cola. I bet The Village Market has some unpetrified
Moon Pies in stock. Did you know that a Moon Pie, placed in
the microwave for just a few seconds is . . . mmmm, a convenience store junkie's gourmet delight? OK, that does it. Got my
own car keys, got my own quarters. I'm outta here. But don't tell
anyone.

I'd really like to get away for a few minutes *all by myself.*

Then shall he have rejoicing in himself alone.
GALATIANS 6:4

Has Anybody Seen Our Brains?

I am not exactly what one might call a Mountain Woman. Or even an Outdoors Woman. Oh, let's be frank here. I'm not even what one could call a Lawn and Garden Woman. And I'm not even remotely what one could call a Ski Buff, Bum, or even Bunny. However, I suppose I could be called a Ski Barely. (Not as in "Skiing Sans Clothing," but as in "Skiing Just Enough to Endanger.")

However, on this Colorado getaway with my husband, Scott, I was—shall we say—feeling my Cheerios. It was late March, and the sun was shining. I was soaking up the joy of this outdoor adventure vacation after having been holed up all winter writing. This tightly wound spring chick had been sprung!

Scott, being of the athletic ilk, enthusiastically encouraged me to try it all: hiking, rock climbing, snow skiing. I am sorry to report that my number-one vigorous outdoor sporting event turned out to be Quaint Little Shop Browsing, but I did engage in a little husband-coerced snow skiing. And it did this middle-aged mother a world of good. With every push of the poles and swish of the snow, my self-esteem climbed. Why, I could almost feel the muscles growing in my biceps and triceps and, yes, even forceps. One might say there's even a little rugged tinge now to my previously ruffled personality.

So when I spied a telephone attached to a tree, right smack in the middle of a nature trail, I was overcome with one desire. I felt compelled to call home and brag—loudly and obnoxiously—to my teenagers. I thought I'd toss out something casual like, "Hey guys, how's it going? Yes, it's your ol' geek mom. Just thought I'd stop on top of this snow peak, gnaw on some beef jerky, and give you guys a quick call before helping your ol' dad down the next slope."

I giggled as I dialed the number, listening impatiently to the rings. It was not one of my teenagers, however, who finally answered the phone. It was my mother, who had graciously volunteered to watch over our four children during our absence. Before I could even say, "Hi, Mom, this is your daughter, Snow Queen of the Mountain," she breathlessly replied, "Oh, Becky, I am *so* glad you called." Then I heard her yell in the background to my fourteen-year-old son, "Zeke! Have you been praying?"

"Mother?" I asked, a little shaken. "What's going on? Are the kids OK?"

"They're fine," she answered quickly, "but we do have a little crisis on our hands."

"What's up?"

"You know Zeke's leaving, in one hour, for that Mexico mission trip with his youth group?"

"Uh-huh."

"Well, a few minutes ago he informed me that he needed a copy of his birth certificate in order to cross the border."

"Oh no!"

Immediately I understood my mother's panic. She knows that if I should die, no living *sane* person could hope to understand my filing system. Without my guidance, she and Zeke would never locate the certificate. But now that I had astutely placed this phone call, everything was *under control.*

Of course, to me, my organization has always made perfect sense. My tax forms are tucked away in a pink rose-covered hat box. (Logic? Put ugly IRS forms in something pretty and feminine. How can one be intimidated by papers in a flowery hat box?) Notes for my books are scattered on pieces of napkins and old envelopes in every room in the house. (I like to surprise myself.) Birth certificates are located—well, your guess is as good as mine. The time my youngest child, Gabriel, needed a birth certificate to get into kindergarten I ended up pleading with the principal to let me drop by and show her my stretch marks instead.

"Becky?"

I was brought back to reality by the way Mother spoke my name, oh so tentatively—I knew she was contemplating all those years she ran around in a mild state of panic, picking up after her absentminded teenage daughter. Now *I* was the mother of my very own absentminded teenager, and my son was in need of a little parental encouragement.

"Mother," I said, "tell Zeke to pick up the phone in my office."

As soon as my mom was safely off the phone and Zeke had picked up the line, I let him have it.

"Son, son, son, son, son! When are you *ever* going to get your act together? I can't believe you've waited until the *last minute* to tell us you needed an important paper! Again! How many times is this going to happen before you realize that you need to think ahead?"

After venting the standard get-your-act-together lecture, I asked my son to follow my careful instructions in order to locate the desired document. After ten minutes of searching, Zeke and Mother methodically dismantled my office until they found (Hallelujah!) the treasured certificate. They finally discovered it in a large brown envelope labeled "Wrist X-Rays." (Logic? Sorry. Even *I'm* stumped on this one.)

Eventually Zeke made the bus to Mexico, and our remaining getaway days in Colorado passed all too quickly. On the plane ride home, Scott and I settled into seats near the rear of the plane. We held hands as we talked about missing the kids, and then laughed and shook our heads over Zeke's near fiasco—confirming once again that we *must* find a way to help our children get their acts together, to teach them to plan ahead, keep up with their things, become more responsible about communication. Otherwise, people would be picking up after them for the rest of their lives. Teenagers!

Just then, a voice broke over the intercom, interrupting our conversation. It was the flight attendant.

"Did anyone on this plane, by any chance, leave a jacket and a red plaid coat in the airport waiting area?"

On the long walk from the back to the front of the airplane to retrieve my belongings, passengers chuckled and picked on me. I played it up, using theatrical gestures and teasing about how I was actually picking up these items for someone else—some crazy, absentminded *friend* of mine. I, of course, had everything *under control.* More laughter broke out up and down the aisle, and then spontaneous bursts of applause.

Ah, well. If I'm not qualified to teach my kids how to get their acts together, perhaps I can at least teach them how to make their acts *entertaining.*

Within a few hours, Scott and I arrived back home in Texas to our children and one kind-hearted but exhausted Granny. After saying our thanks and good-byes, we sent my mother on her way—for the hour-and-a-half drive back to her home near Dallas. She wanted to leave in plenty of time to meet my father for lunch before he flew off on a business trip to Canada.

Later that evening we received a phone call delivered via a French-sounding telephone operator who put us through to my father. Even through the fuzzy connection Daddy's voice sounded worried. He went on to explain that Mother had never shown up for their lunch date. He had gone ahead with his trip, expecting she would call him later to explain her delay. But he'd never heard from her, and she had not answered the phone all day. Had we heard anything?

We had not.

The circumstances grew more and more suspect. Her close friends had not heard anything. Neighbors were alerted. The health club where she faithfully performs her daily workout said she had not signed in. ("Oh, yes," they said, "we know your mother well. She's the one that comes in to walk the treadmill in her high heels and handbag." Obviously, my athletic genes did not fall far from my mother's tree.)

At this point I begged Scott to call the police and area hospitals. In the meantime, we also telephoned Mother's best friend, Almedia, who happened to have a key to Mother's house. She volunteered to drive over and check out the circumstances. Within minutes, she'd called us back.

"Scott and Becky, I'm a little boggled here. All the lights are on, the television is blaring, and groceries are on the counter, still in their bags."

"Scott!" I yelled hysterically. "My mother's been kidnapped!"

About that time, Mother walked through her front door, totally unaware of the panic she'd left in her wake and shocked by the sight of Almedia sitting in her house using her telephone. As it turned out, Mother had been delayed by traffic and had decided, as long as she wasn't going to make her lunch date with Dad, to take in an afternoon matinee. It had been her understanding that the lunch date with Daddy was more of a loose we'll-do-lunch-if-I-can-make-it-back-in-time sort of an arrangement.

Once we knew Mother was all right—and after shedding a few tears of relief—Scott and I sat down at the kitchen counter and sighed. He was the first to speak. "I tell ya, Becky, these fifty-nine-year-olds think they can just take off gallivanting around the country without letting a soul know their whereabouts!"

"I know," I replied, resting my chin in resignation on my palm. "It's totally irresponsible, that's what it is."

Then simultaneously, we both smiled and asked each other, "When do you think our parents are ever going to get their act together?"

A few days later, Mother and I reunited over a cup of mocha latte at Hav-a-Java.

"Mother," I said, "I can't believe I blew up at *Zeke* for being irresponsible. Then within twenty-four hours, *I'm* being paged—to the front of an airplane, like some unruly girl, for not keeping up with my things. Then *you* have the *entire city* in a panic because you neglected to tell anyone about your change in plans."

"Well, Beck," my mother replied, sipping at the foam rising over the top of her cup, "look at the bright side. These events really close the generation gap—because it sure seems to me that kids, parents, and even grandparents have at least one thing in common: None of us have our acts *altogether* together."

"Yep, you're right," I sighed, stirring my coffee. "And anyway, if we ever do get it together in this family, I have a funny feeling we'd just forget where we put it!"

For you were like sheep going astray.
1 PETER 2:25
&

Will You Go *with* Me?

A magazine caught my eye the other day. And even though it's so politically correct it is nauseating, I bought it because the cover intrigued me. On the front was a photograph of a little boy and girl, both dressed in grown-up attire: business suits, briefcases, the whole bit. The question across the top of the picture asked, "Are you grown-up yet?" Then, in parentheses, it also asked, "Do you know anyone who is?" I don't quite know how to answer those questions. I think it depends on your definition of the word *grown-up*.

If grown-up means that you have your own quarters and can eat dessert first, hey, I'm as adult as they come. If being grown-up means you can snow ski, I'm now snow plowing with the Big Dogs. (I'm still pretty proud of this.) But if, by any chance, being grown-up means you are a responsible, competent out-of-town traveler, bring me my blankie and a pacifier.

Middle-age has brought so many "firsts" my way. (Why doesn't the above-thirty crowd get baby books—with blanks to fill in for our First Gray Hair, First Pair of Bifocals, First Hot Flash, and so on?) One of the biggest challenges and changes in my life is that I've become a real, live author; and because of this, I'm getting some invitations to travel and give real, live speeches. The first obstacle I had to overcome was my fear of flying. Of course, it wasn't so much that I was afraid of *flying;* it was the *falling* part that always got to me. But I'm much, much better. (In my imaginary baby book I could sign and date a category for First Airplane Trip Accomplished without Embedding Finger-nails into Arm of Passenger Sitting Next to Me.)

The second hurdle has not been as easy for me to jump. Because of what Gabe so succinctly pointed out at the start of this book—the part about my having no sense—out-of-state travel poses a special challenge. There are a few basic skills that would, I'm sure, increase my confidence level as I try finding my way around a strange city—for instance, the ability to read a map.

I've been blessed thus far to have friends who are so desperate to get away they've been willing to take me on as a traveling companion. Little did they know what they were committing themselves to. My problem with traveling is this: Once I hit the airport, I transform—responsibility speaking—to a child of about five years old. Thus, the person traveling with me begins a subtle development into the parent.

Tina Jacobson was one of my first traveling buddies. Tina owns a burgeoning home-based business called Books and Bookings, and has arranged all the radio publicity for my books. The first time we ever talked on the phone, we hit it off and since have become good friends. We even make regular lunch dates to discuss publishing and marketing, and wife-ing and mothering, and what it is like to try to operate a professional business with kids wandering in and out of our offices asking, "What's for din-ner?" So when we both had business to conduct in Nashville, Tina agreed to go with me to help me learn the ropes of travel savvy.

I met her at the Dallas-Fort Worth airport. When it was our turn to board the plane, Tina asked, "Becky, now where is your ticket?" Already, her voice had picked up a faint maternal quality.

"It's in my purse. Don't worry," I replied with a grin.

"OK," said Tina. "Don't get offended by this, but I *have* read your books. Where is your purse?"

"Well, it is right—*oh no!* I don't know! Oh, my goodness, it has over three hundred dollars in cash and my airplane ticket in it!"

Tina swallowed hard, checked her watch, and then asked me very carefully where I had been in the last few minutes.

"The rest room! I was in the ladies' room!"

Running full speed ahead I darted to the ladies' room and there—miraculously—sitting in the sink was my open purse. Right where I'd left it. Not one penny was missing. I praised God from the top of my lungs and caught up with Tina just in time to board the plane.

I learned my lesson right away and held on to my purse from then on, as if my life depended on it. I did very well, too, until we went out to eat at a restaurant in Nashville. We had a delicious dinner, and as we turned to leave, I double-checked to make sure I had my purse swinging over my shoulder. Then Tina asked calmly, "Are you missing anything?"

"Nope," I answered, with childlike confidence. "See, I've got my purse right here. My head is attached to my body. Everything is *under control.*"

"Why don't you check under the table, just in case."

And there, where I had been sitting, lay five twenty-dollar bills.

"Oops," I apologized, sheepishly retrieving the cash off the floor. "Guess I should start *zipping up* my purse, huh?"

"Becky," Tina asked as we started to leave, "you *are* older than me, right?"

"Yeah, by a couple of years, I think."

"Then why do I suddenly feel like your mother?"

"Don't worry. This always happens when I go on trips with people. I should have warned you."

"Well, then, I must ask: Do you need to go potty before we leave?"

My next willing travel victim was my neighbor from the boonies, Melissa. Our first out-of-town trip started off smoothly enough. We boarded the plane without a hitch, laughing and talking the entire first leg of the journey. However, the challenge began when we had to pick up our luggage before changing planes in Phoenix. We retrieved our bags without a problem, but then we had to descend an escalator—and both of us were loaded to the neck with luggage. I do not know what possessed Melissa to do this, but she insisted I go first.

When I reached the bottom of the escalator, I managed to step off fairly gracefully. Unfortunately, my suitcase was heavier than I realized and I couldn't drag it off with me. There it sat, like a road block, stuck on the bottom step. Which meant that Melissa had to descend the escalator with bags under each arm and *straddle* my suitcase to keep from tripping over it and falling on her face. She was also, I might add, wearing a dress.

This scene—like something out of an "I Love Lucy" rerun—struck me as *hilarious.* Unfortunately, when I get really, really tickled, something horrible happens: I become completely incapacitated. I was literally sprawled on the airport floor, laughing so hard that tears were falling down both cheeks. Melissa, on the other hand, did not seem to find the situation quite as amusing. That's when she began to adopt the mother role.

"Get up off that floor and come help me!" she ordered. (I really expected her to add, "young lady!")

Eventually, I pulled myself up and managed to offer some weak assistance. Thankfully it didn't take long for Melissa to get tickled, too, and she forgave me. From there, our trip went relatively smoothly until the airplane ride home. I boarded the plane with several pieces of take-on luggage and one shopping bag full of huge cinnamon rolls, each of them the size of a cantaloupe. We'd promised our children a treat, and these monster rolls seemed the perfect answer. As we were squeezing down the aisle, trying to locate our seats, the bottom of my shopping bag broke loose.

"Uh-oh," I said quietly. Melissa's eyes widened with disbelief. Like a dozen bowling balls gone wild, the cinnamon rolls began veering crazily down the alley and under the seats, with passengers yelling, "Catch that big roll coming toward you!" and "There goes one under your feet!" Melissa looked at the flight attendant and rolled her eyes upward. As I scrambled around on my hands and knees, I believe I overheard Melissa say, "Kids! Whadaya gonna do with 'em?"

A year later, Melissa's memories of traveling with me had faded somewhat, and besides, she was desperate to break loose from the boonies again. This time, we were heading to sunny California. We adopted our Lucy and Ethel roles right away, humming bars of "California, Here We Come" as we stepped off our plane at John Wayne Airport. After I finished my speaking engagement, we checked ourselves into a budget hotel and spent the next few days doing the tourist thing: Universal Studios (where we lingered for an hour at the "Tribute to Lucy" display), Mann's Chinese Theater (where I had my picture taken with John Wayne's boot prints), and Beverly Hills (where we ate lunch and gawked). Amazingly, I managed to behave like a responsible adult the entire trip, and Melissa was even able to relax. Well, almost.

Our budget hotel turned out to be the epitome of economy (the swimming pool was the size of my kitchen table), but we did get an in-room whirlpool bathtub. And after a long day of touristing, I was eager to give that whirlpool a whirl. So I flipped a switch on the wall, positioned myself in the tub, laid back, and let the steaming water pour in. I couldn't wait to feel those little scrubbing bubbles work their magic on my aching muscles.

Then something unusual happened. Something for which I was totally unprepared. Water began shooting out of the little holes on the side of the tub like a fountain. As a matter of fact, the jets began propelling eight-foot streams of water upward and all around me, hitting the walls, the ceiling, soaking the floor. And then, that horrible thing happened again. I got tickled. I could not move; I could not speak. I could hear Melissa pounding on the door, but I could not answer her. All I could do was cuddle up in a ball and snicker and snort.

"Becky! Answer me!" Melissa was yelling outside the bathroom door. "Are you OK? I hear something splatting against the wall! Becky! There is *water* pouring out from under the *door!*"

Still I could not catch my breath as I sat like one of those cherub statues encased in a huge fountain of water. The noise of the whirlpool drowned out my feeble attempts to communicate. Finally, Melissa opened the door a couple of inches. Streams of water hit her—splat—in the face. As a matter of fact, the water shot out so hard and so high that it arched over her head, soaking one of the headboards and bedspreads out in the *room!*

"I won't look," promised Melissa as her arm stretched toward the whirlpool button on the wall, "but I'm coming in and turning this thing off!"

Immediately, the indoor hurricane died down and we surveyed the damage. An inch of water puddled on the floor, and beads of water dripped from every conceivable surface. The towels were useless—completely saturated. Melissa smoothed a lock of damp hair off her forehead. The maternal voice returned. "Becky, did you read the instructions?"

"What instructions?"

"The ones on the bathtub that say, *first* fill the tub up with water until it covers the jets. *Then* turn the whirlpool button on."

"Oh, *those* instructions."

Melissa made me promise not to touch any more buttons without her permission. For "tomorrow, if I were very, very good," she said she'd to take me with her to Disneyland!

> *Entreat me not to leave thee, or to return from*
> *following after thee: for whither thou goest,*
> *I will go; and where thou lodgest, I will lodge.*
>
> RUTH 1:16, KJV

135

Is There Really
a Magic Kingdom?

Walt Disney once said, "I myself have been flattered by the reputation for never having quite grown up."[12] And I must say, having recently visited Mr. Disney's fantasy world, this reputation seems pretty accurate to me.

Though you walk through the gates of Disney's Magic Kingdom an adult, everyone comes out a child on the other side. Melissa and I flew above rooftops in Never, Neverland. We sat entranced at the intricate detail and diversity of the famous "It's a Small World" ride. (Though I believe if I had to hear the chorus of that repetitive song one more time, I might go out of my small, small mind.) I wondered, perplexed, at the new virtual reality rides: I mean, how do they *do* that? How do they make you feel as though you've just sped through galaxies in a star ship?

But my favorite part of all was the parade. Not just any parade, but the Lion King Parade—Disney style. Never in all my life have I seen such a gorgeous display, such beautiful music, right where I could reach out and touch it. I found myself caught up in it all. I was incredibly moved as dancers of all nationalities in brilliant costumes ascended poles and floats and swayed to the beautiful rhythms of the song "The Circle of Life."

By evening, I was a grinning fool, sporting a Mickey Mouse shirt and a matching beanie complete with propeller.

"Melissa," I said to my friend as we stopped for a rest and a bite to eat, "I've been suckered into this whole commercial theme park deal. Look at me! Can you believe it? I've bought the entire enchilada."

"I noticed," said Melissa, aiming a camera in my direction. "It happens to the best of us. You've been thoroughly Disneyed."

We found a table near a jazz band and dance floor and propped our weary feet on a nearby chair. The band started up, playing the romantic, toe-tapping music of the 1940s era. Melissa and I visited with some teenagers during the break, who were elegantly dressed in forties regalia. They'd been having a ball, swing-stepping together under the stars. A new trend among teens? I hope so. They told us they come out several times a week just for some good, wholesome fun. (I know, you could have knocked us over with a feather, too.)

The breeze was soft around my face. The gentle wind-caress gave me a twinge of homesickness. I wished—OK, yes, *upon a star*—that my husband could have been there with me at that moment. He'd have had me out on that dance floor in no time. And we'd have given those young whippersnappers a run for their money.

From the corner of my eye, I could see a young father buying his little boy some ice cream. The child reached up for the cone, his chubby hand eager for the cold, dripping sweetness. Then the band, in the background, began playing what is, perhaps, my favorite song. Slow and sweet, its melody melted the simple smile of the evening into my memory. For I believe Louis Armstrong captured for all time the essence of childlike joy when he flashed his famous grin and gifted us with "What a Wonderful World."

As the last strains of the music wound down, the little boy finished off his last bite of ice cream. Then just as the crooner sang the final, "What—a-won-der-ful—world," the child—as if on cue—clapped his sticky hands together, grinned for all he was worth, looked straight at me, and shouted, "Yeah!" And I looked at him and shouted, "Yeah!" right back at him. And for that enchanted moment, connecting on some special frequency with this child, the world indeed seemed sparkling and amazing and completely wonderful. Louis would have been pleased.

Ironically, I understand some people have called for a boycott of Disney. There is cause for concern. Disney, the multi-million-dollar company, has certainly wandered far from the type of entertainment that Walt Disney, the creator, originally envisioned for children and their parents to enjoy together. But I have some personal misgivings about the value of boycotts. I believe it is usually more effective to spend our time lighting candles than shouting at the darkness—throwing more effort into applauding what is beautiful and right rather than acting appalled when man does what man-without-God will naturally do. But that's just my Mickey Mouse opinion.

I've been pondering something since my day at Disneyland: I noticed it is *grown-ups* who buy the tickets for their *children* to enter into the Magic Kingdom. Parents are the ones who drive the little tikes there, guide the way through the gates, and take them on the rides. But in the kingdom of God, according to Jesus, the roles are reversed. It is the *children* who point the way for us grown-ups to enter in to all the Kingdom's riches: humbly, delightedly, and wholeheartedly.

Part of the Kingdom can be experienced here and now as we ride the roller coaster of life—from infancy, to toddlerhood, to grade school, adolescence, young adulthood, middle-age, and old age. Depending on the Creator of it all to teach us, to help us, to love us, to comfort us around each curve, each bend, each thrill, and each terror.

And then, one day, the roller coaster will plunge into that mysterious dark Tunnel of Death. But death is only a temporary door—opening and birthing us into a magnificent world beyond our wildest dreams. "Yes," I can tell my children, "there really is a Magic Kingdom."

Sometimes, when I'm all alone, I try to imagine what that Kingdom might be like. Surely delighted giggles of children will be among the parade of singing angels as we gather around our King's throne. And I think to myself, *What a wonderful world.*

But Jesus called the children to Him and said,
"Let the little children come to me,
and do not hinder them,
for the kingdom of God belongs to such as these.
I tell you the truth, anyone who will not receive
the kingdom of God like a little child
will never enter it."
LUKE 18:16–17

Can You Come Tuck Me In?

"Nighty-night, sleep tight. And don't let the bedbugs bite."

How many of us were tucked in bed and left with this parental sign-off ringing in our ears as we lay in the darkness? I loved it, but why I loved it I can't quite fathom. Interpreted literally this night-night farewell says, basically, "Sweet dreams my little one—by the way, I'd keep a sharp eye out for biting insects crawling under the covers if I were you." How did a message that sounds like it sprung from a twisted mind end up part of our "comforting" bedtime routines?

Perhaps this is only one example of many pre-bedtime activities that elude all logic. Back when the children were tiny, we had quite the involved bedtime routine. I read to them, bathed them, rocked them, sang to them, prayed with them, nursed and/or watered them, diapered and/or pottied them, hugged them, kissed them, and stopped often to gaze at them—cute as baby bunnies in their soft feety pajamas. Then I repeated many of these things several more times throughout the evening before they actually fell asleep. By that time, I was wiped out—too exhausted even to cry, much less marvel over how cute they were. So why, thinking about it now, do I suddenly miss it all?

As I ponder childhood bedtime rituals, I realize that I still have several of my own nighty-night traditions I've carried into adulthood. Almost every night, I grab a good book or magazine and head to my tub full of hot-as-I-can-stand-it water. When I've steamed and read long enough that my eyes refuse to decode another word and my toes have turned into ten wrinkly prunes, I know I'm preheated and ready for bed. Once snuggled under the covers, I spoon into the curve of my sleeping husband and drop contentedly off to sleep. Unless my sleeping husband is just pretending and not actually ready for full-fledged sleep. But I . . . um, digress.

As far back as I can remember, a hot bath, a good book, and snuggling up (with a pillow or comforter in the days before Scott was handy) have been part of my nightly routine. On the other hand, Scott has his own method of going off to dreamland. As soon as he realizes it is a proper time to retire, he stumbles toward the bedroom, peeling off excess garments, and *while* he is actually plummeting toward the bed, he falls asleep—mid-air—before his head hits the pillow. It never ceases to amaze me.

As one might imagine, our diverse bedtime routines have also been the cause of some ongoing conflict. Not long ago, after a rough night's sleep, we tried to discuss our sleeping preferences rationally. I opened the debate.

"Scott, I understand that you like to have some fresh air coming in the room. All I'm asking is that it not be of the arctic variety. I honestly think I saw snow flurries drifting out of the air vents last night."

"Becky," Scott calmly replied, "just because your feet never thaw does not mean the rest of us like to sleep with the temperature set on broil. What you need to do is tuck your head under the covers, like me, and you'll be warm as toast."

"I can't! It makes me claustrophobic. Look, I'm gasping for air just thinking about it." I clutched at my throat for effect.

"Do you think you could possibly be a little more melodramatic?"

"And besides, O Toasty One, you wouldn't even let me warm my feet on your calves last night."

"That's because you kept pinching my leg hairs with your toes."

"OK. Let's move on to the next subject. What I want to know is why you and the kids go so ballistic whenever a teensy, weensy shred of light slithers its way into your rooms?"

"Shred of light? *Shred of light?* Beck, you leave so many lights on in the house every night, the neighbors must think we never sleep. Which isn't too far from the truth. The only thing we're lacking is a rotating searchlight in each closet!"

"Now who's being dramatic? Look, I *need* lights on in the house so I can see my way to the children should they need me in case of fire. Or a burglar. Or a stomach virus."

"That's ridiculous."

"Yeah, well obviously you've never groped in the darkness for a nauseous child. Believe me, mister, it only takes once."

There is no end in sight to these debates. Amazingly, I keep loving Scott in spite of his weird habits. (It's so nice to be the one in charge of the slant this book takes.) Somehow we've managed to get in at least a few hours of sleep each night for the past twenty years.

As I'm writing this, it is after 10:00 P.M. Fighting off yawns, I'm still in my office taking advantage of the unusual quiet, but I'm not completely alone. Zeke is in an easy chair beside me, silently reading his homework assignment. Zachary, our eldest, just opened the door to "check and see if Zeke was ready for bed yet." The boys still share a room (they have no choice). *Their* bedtime routine consists of listening to music, discussing stuff they think adults are too old to understand, and arguing about whose turn it is to turn off the light.

Zachary looked so forlorn just now, peeking his head around the door, dressed in his boxer shorts and baggy T-shirt. I couldn't resist teasing him a bit. "Poor Zachary," I said in my syrupy-mommy voice. "Can't you get off to sleep without your little brother and your nighty-night pillow talk?" Zach stifled a sheepish grin while unconvincingly denying my charge. He's already checked on Zeke once more to see if he was "done yet." Despite Zach's protests, it's obvious that he enjoys his nightly chats with his brother.

Scott and I usually have our pillow talk before he goes to bed. Unless I'm simply in the mood to hear myself chattering a soliloquy, I have to catch my husband before he begins the descent toward his pillow. Thankfully, I still get a chance to enjoy a little pillow talk with the youngest children, Rachel and Gabe. My Rachel, bless her heart, can always be counted on for a nightly hug and kiss and quickie chat. And to her everlasting credit, she'll even come to find me before heading to bed instead of relying on her absentminded mother to remember to tuck her in.

Then there's Gabe, the Champion Pillow Talker of the Western World. If only I had more time to lie down with Gabe before he drifted off to sleep, I could gather enough material to keep me writing for a lifetime.

During one of our recent going-off-to-bed talks, I discovered Gabriel has an unusual, secret nightlife. During the ages when most kids are supposed to be afraid of the dark, I discovered that Gabe was actually roaming from room to room, where he would collect things from underneath the beds of his sleeping siblings. He was, simply put, a nocturnal treasure hunter.

"Gabe," I asked in surprise, "aren't you afraid to put your hand under a bed at night?" Psychologically speaking, I know that's a dysfunctional question for a parent to ask a kid— especially a child so obviously well-adjusted to the dark. But as a little girl, I used to be petrified of the make-believe alligators roaming under my bed. I was sure they hid there every night, waiting for an opportunity to snack on my toes or hands. Remembering this, the question slipped out before I thought better of it. In any case, I needn't have worried. Gabe simply looked at me as if I'd lost my mind.

"No, Mom! Are you kidding? You can get some really good stuff under there." As proof, he showed me his stash: a tennis ball, a pile of rubber bands, an old piece of candy, and a Frisbee. He went on to say that he also talked to his drapes at night, pretending they were his friend. "Oh, really?" I asked him. "Do you have a name for your little imaginary friend?" Of course he did. How silly of me to ask. His friend's name was "Curtain."

There is no telling what we might learn about the intriguing private worlds of our wee ones if we lingered a little longer at the edges of their beds. Or as they grow up and their bedtimes begin to outlast ours, I think teenagers should be obligated to come to tuck *us* into bed. And, since turnabout is fair play, we parents ought to refuse to go to sleep until they bring us three or four drinks of water, read us a story, sing us a song, rub our backs, listen to our pillow talk, and help us say our goodnight prayers.

Well, it's bedtime. And I've spent my "pillow talk" moments with you, my reader friend, tonight. So to all a good night. Please do sleep tight. And even though I think it might be psychologically destructive to say this—don't let the bedbugs bite.

I will lie down and sleep in peace, for you alone,
O LORD, make me dwell in safety.
PSALM 4:8
❧

I'm Just Fixin' Stuff

L ate tonight, after a long day of playing handyman around the house, Scott plopped his tired body down in the old green rocker in my office. Ever since he was a little boy, Scott has been "fixin' stuff." And Lord help the woman who ever so much as suggests he might hire a professional. Fixin' stuff is my man's sacred territory—*his* boyish realm of "I can do it all by myself."

For a few seconds Scott just sat and rocked, grateful for a respite, as I finished some editing. I typed in the last correction, swiveled my chair around, and propped my feet up on my husband's weary knees.

"Tired?" I asked.

"Exhausted," he answered, staring blankly ahead.

"So now that you are here, I suppose you'd better go ahead and tell me the news. Do we have water? And if we do, is it hot, cold, or lukewarm? And, I'm almost afraid to ask but . . ." I gazed upward at this point, my hands folded together. "Lord have mercy on us, do we have a clothes dryer yet?" I crossed my fingers and shut my eyes tight as I waited in suspense for the reply.

I should explain that for three weeks now, we've been without a clothes dryer. Actually, we've always been without a *legitimate* clothes dryer. I bought the machine used—well used—from a local laundromat for the bargain price of twenty dollars. For our "twenty big ones" we got a harvest gold machine that looked and sounded more like an enormous rock tumbler than a clothes dryer.

In the beginning, the dryer sounded as if it were tossing, say, a few small pebbles. Then it went through a period of time when the pebble-tumbling noises actually came to a halt—which would have been a relief, except that our mechanically deranged friend had other tricks up its belts. At this point our clothes tumbler went from merely drying our clothes, to baking them. Honestly. White dress shirts began popping out of the steel door the color of perfectly browned toast. During this awkward stage of dryerhood our clothes always smelled suspiciously as if they'd been dried at the end of a coat hanger over a campfire.

Finally, Scott figured out how to adjust the temperature from bake/broil to normal, but then the rock-tumbling noises started again. Only this time, the sound had graduated from mere namby-pamby pebble tumbling to serious boulder grinding. We knew our dryer's days were numbered when Jim Ed, our next-door neighbor, came over and asked Scott if we could hear the horrible noise our "air conditioner" was making outside. (I love the way folks out here get some use out of the middle names. Jim Ed's my favorite, but we also know and love Mary Sue, Ida Lou, and Sue Ann.) Scott had to confess that the ruckus Jim Ed had heard was not emitting from an outside air conditioner unit, but our inside clothes dryer. I was sure it would blow at any moment, but for several more weeks it noisily, but efficiently, managed to keep drying our clothes. Finally, the hunk of metal clanked to a grinding halt. But hey, we figured we had squeezed our twenty bucks out of it.

You aren't going to believe this, but about six months ago, we had actually purchased a nice, almost new, dryer. It's been sitting on my back porch just waiting for the old machine to give up the ghost so it could move in on its territory. *Why in the world,* one might be wondering, *did we wait so long to replace Old Yeller?*

I'll tell you why. Because the new, improved dryer must run on propane. And before we could install it, for reasons only completely understood by my husband, we would have to let our butane tank temporarily run out of fuel. *Why?* So he could move the tank over to the side of the house. *Oh.* And if he was going to move the butane tank over to the side of the house, he would also like to go ahead and move the water tank from the bathroom to the laundry room. *I hope this makes sense to you.* And if he had to do that, well then, all sorts of plumbing lines and gizmos and connectors and such would have to be moved and welded and soldered and piped. This could take days, Scott had been ominously predicting. Faced with this scenario, I agreed with my husband that the most logical thing to do under the circumstances was, of course, to stall—as long as humanly possible. This weekend, however, the jig was up.

For the last four days—in addition to air drying our laundry on the back porch like a family of hillbillies—we've also been coping without benefit of hot water—in January.

Over this weekend I've not seen either of Scott's hands without tools attached to them, and I've only caught brief glimpses of his face from behind bars and under pipes. He's grown the scraggly beginnings of a beard. His eyes have taken on a hollow, haunted look and all his attempts at conversation have started with, "Becky, please tell me you've seen a little piece of metal that looks like an elbow," or "a donut," or "your grandfather's nose."

"Becky," he confessed at one point, "I think I've had my fill of fixing stuff now."

"Do you want me to hire a—"

"Don't say it! Don't even *think* it. Give me time. I'll get my second wind."

And me? Oh, I've been pressing bravely on. I've devised an ingenious system, I think, for still managing to get my daily hot bath. I can go without almost anything, but anyone who knows me well, knows I will *not* be deprived of my daily hot soak in the tub. My system?

First, I begin by putting four of my biggest pots on the stove top to boil (we have an electric stove, thank goodness, that is unaffected by the empty butane tank), and then I heat one big bowl of water in the microwave.

Then I take off all my clothes (so as not to waste precious time when the stage is set), wrap a towel around me, and shuffle back and forth from the kitchen to the bathroom until I've emptied three gallons of boiling water into the bathtub. (Of course, the neighborhood kids have been a little curious. "Hey, what's your mom cookin' up in the bathroom? Does she always wear a towel when she boils water?")

Then I refill the pots, set them all back on the stove to boil again, and jump in the tub before the water cools off. Midway through my bath, when my hair is all lathered up with shampoo, I pop out of the tub, repeat the running back and forth with hot pads and pots of boiling water, in order to reheat the two inches of bathwater that have now begun to cool.

Just call me Pioneer Woman. If I am anything, I am adaptable.

So now you understand how much I had vested in the answers I was about to receive from my bone-weary husband. The news was mixed.

"Becky," he began solemnly, as if he were giving a battle brief, "as it now lines up—yes, we have a working clothes dryer."

"Hallelujah!"

"Yes, there is hot and cold running water in the bathtub."

"That's my little handyman! I knew you could do it!"

"However, there is no water at all in any of the bathroom sinks."

"Yuuuuck . . . "

"In the kitchen, I have hot water only coming out of the faucet."

"That I can live with."

"No water to the dishwasher."

"That I cannot. What about the washing machine?"

"Cold only."

"All in all, sir," I replied with a dutiful salute, "not too shabby. The troops will survive. For a couple of days. But I cannot write another word tonight. May I be dismissed now? I have an appointment with a tub of steaming hot water."

The next morning.

It was rather amusing this morning to watch the kids fighting over who got to use the bathtub first—to brush their teeth and wet their combs. I went to the kitchen sink for a cold drink of water and forgot that today's option from that particular faucet was limited to hot liquids only. Resigned, I put a tea bag in a cup of steaming water from the hydrant and let it steep. Then I sat down on my living room couch—the only neat, new piece of furniture we've ever bought—and began a melancholy muse.

Sometimes I think our lives are so very strange—surely I'm stuck in an ongoing sitcom from the Twilight Zone. Or maybe we're really on Perpetual Candid Camera.

I can't help it. Sometimes, I confess, I compare. Not our family's lifestyle to other people's, really—at least not often. What I compare is my neat, clean suburban upbringing to this wacky, country, live-by-the-seat-of-our-pants life we are giving our children. I do laugh about it. This house-building project provided much of the inspiration for my first three books.

We still chuckle at the time when we'd first moved to this dilapidated cabin and our Gabriel, at about age three, grabbed his coat and started out the door. When we asked him where he was going, he answered, "I'm goin' home now." I informed him that this new "house" was now our home. That's when Gabe cried out—on behalf of us all, really—"But this house is broken!" However, I would not change our decision to move to the country, building as we could afford, even if I could. But I'll be honest; there are times when it gets awfully tough.

My mind drifts back to an evening two weeks ago. . . .

I am sitting at my big, round kitchen table. The dining room set is used furniture, too, of course; I found it at a bargain shop.

But I love this table with its nicks and character lines. It's a deep honey-colored maple, like the Early American furniture you see in old magazines from the fifties. It's a table meant for turkey and stuffing and coffee and cookies and family and conversation. Norman Rockwell would have loved my table, I think. But this evening, there are no turkeys or chocolate chip cookies on my honey-colored table. Instead, the maple surface is covered with bills, bills, and more bills. I *hate* bills.

We've come so, so far. We really have. From a one-bedroom cabin to a gorgeous two-story shell, at least, of a home. Built, every board, by my husband, with occasional help from his sons. In the last few months, Scott & Sons have managed to finish our beautiful living room—giving us much-needed space for our sprawling family. But still, on this night of bills, Scott and I admit we are not where we had hoped we'd be at this point in time. We face the possibility of not being able to give our children what we so desperately want them to have before it is too late and they are grown and gone. Our fixer-upper might not get fixed. Zach's best chance at a room of his own may be a college dorm. Still, my husband refuses to dig deeper into debt to finish the house. In my heart I know he is right. But this is hard truth, still, for me to swallow.

Our oldest son and his brother still share a small room. Gabriel sleeps in a makeshift hall. Rachel must crawl over Gabriel's bed to get to her bedroom. My kitchen cabinets are held up by a two-by-four. There's still only one bathroom for the six of us. These things eat at us—the parents, the *providers*.

Sometimes I wonder if they bother me even more than Scott, though I know he agonizes too. But Scott was the youngest in his family, and his household was, for most of his life, in some state of remodeling flux. His dad was ever the tinkerer in his off hours, and his mom the creative type—knocking down walls on a whim, redecorating with antiques and sentimental finds. It honestly never bothered Scott that his bedroom was, for a few years, a walk-in closet. His parents have a lovely home on a lake now, but it is ever-evolving into new form too.

———

My parents, on the other hand, were the typical seventies couple who bought into the concept of new, neat, simple: the gift-boxed suburban dream on a cul-de-sac. Perhaps I feel the guilt about the state of our home more acutely because it contrasts so sharply with what I knew as a child.

By the time I was in third grade I had a large, bright bedroom of my own with new ruffled white curtains and sunny yellow furniture. The carpet matched and flowed smoothly from one room to another. We had two bathrooms and a huge kitchen with built-in coppertone appliances. There were two living areas, a laundry room, a two-car garage, and a bedroom to house each sibling, along with my parents' master bedroom. The paint was fresh, the caulk was neat, the trim all finished. It was such a neat little package. I even had a neat little yard, with real grass that got mowed and watered, and a porch swing and a fence. Today, my parents own a similar home—only prettier, neater, more polished, and beautifully decorated.

I have to admit, though, even as a child growing up in a "perfect house," I dreamed of living in the country, with woods and water and picket fences all around. I'd ride my bike out away from the subdivisions until I found myself a tree to climb or a pond to read by.

My husband breaks my reverie, sitting down beside me at the table and pouring me a cup of coffee. Then, one by one, our children file in from the front door and from various rooms in the house and join us around our table. As if by instinct, they seem to know I need their strength. The coffee and my family softens the sight of the monster bills. Then Scott speaks.

"Kids," he says, "we love you guys. We moved to the country because we chose to give you nature and water and woods over a nice, modern home. Sometimes we wonder if we've done the right thing. And I want you to know that your mother and I want more than anything to finish this house. We want you to each have a bedroom of your own and we all want the privacy an extra bathroom would give us. I want your mom to drive a decent car. But I refuse to go deeper into debt. Times, right now, are a little tighter than they've been for a while. We need to slow down our spending, and we need you guys to be understanding."

One by one, each of our children offers words of comfort. "Mom and Dad, you've given us a great life." "Dad, we're not in a big hurry. We're OK." "Look at our beautiful living room! At least now there's room for parties and kids to come over and spend the night on the floor." "We'd rather live like this and be in the country any day than one of those perfect houses in the city."

The tears fall freely down my face. Scott takes my hand and offers his other hand to the child beside him. One by one each brother or sister takes the hand of the other until the circle closes. Then Scott prays for us to be satisfied and grateful, as a family, for what God has given us. Out-loud prayers are not frequent occurrences in our family—other than at mealtime. It means the world to me that my husband senses I need this. Maybe moments like these are what growing up is all about.

Later, Scott catches me in the hall and says, "Becky, Zachary just offered to sell his car if it would help out. Maybe we came across a little too pitiful. But we've got a good bunch of kids, don't we?"

I nod slowly. We are wealthy.

Back to early this morning . . .

Comforted by that memory, I got up from the couch, walked out the front door, and could hardly believe my eyes. There, in front of God and the neighbors and everybody, sat a white commode. As columnist Dave Barry is prone to say, I am *not* making this up. I did an about-face and marched back into the house.

"Look, Scott," I stated in no uncertain terms, "I'm a very patient woman. But this is where I draw the line! I'm OK with table saws and towers of pink insulation stacked on my front porch. I can even handle a dryer on the back porch. But I refuse—for even one second—to have a *potty* in my front yard!"

"Gee, Becky," Scott said calmly, "I just needed to spray it off. No need to cry about it!"

"Hey, Buster, it's my potty and I'll cry if I want to!"

One look at my face and he knew I'd reached my limit. As the kids and I loaded up in the station wagon for the drive to their school, I saw Scott run out the front door (in nothing but his boxer shorts), pick up the commode, and drag it to the front porch. Then he threw a blanket over it, in a futile attempt at camouflage.

Zeke couldn't resist a comment. "Hey, Dad, try putting a hat on it!"

I finally got tickled and hollered out, "And a carrot nose and corncob pipe!" Scott just grinned and darted back in the house.

He is taking off a few days to work on the house and get it in shape for Friday night when the kids' youth group comes over for a game night and pizza party. Hopefully, all our faucets will be running hot and cold again by then. (If not, it is safe to assume that my blood will be.)

Learning to be content with where we are and with what we have is one of the most difficult lessons I'm having to learn. In reading through a little book called *Kids Say the Greatest Things about God,* I came across a child's interpretation of heaven that my children could probably "Amen." The little boy said, "When you get your room in heaven, you don't have to share it with any of your brothers. Or, if you do have to share, God makes it so you don't mind sharing."[13]

It is a child, once again, that puts life back in perspective for me. Nothing will ever be "just right" here on earth. It isn't really supposed to be. But one day we'll have a home that is absolutely perfect, where everything is working—or even if it isn't, God will make it so I won't mind. And Scott, I'm sure, will be tinkering on the mansions—having the time of his life just "fixin' stuff."

I have learned to be satisfied
with the things I have
and with everything that happens.

I know how to live when I am poor.
And I know how to live when I have plenty.
I have learned the secret of being happy
at any time in everything that happens.
PHILIPPIANS 4:11–12, NCV

❧

Let's Go Muddin'!

Mud . . . glorious mud.

Remember the feel of squish-squashy stuff oozing up between your toes? Who knows how many chefs began their careers by decorating fancy mud pies with chocolate dirt and candy rocks and twig candles. When asked what God did with His time, one youngster replied, "God makes bees with little wings all day. Probably out of mud."[14] Since God created Adam from the dust of the earth, this child must have concluded that God continues to create masterpieces from dirt, eternally up to His elbows in mud. Who knows?

I'd almost forgotten what wonderful amusement a bit of dirt and water can provide for a child. And how *large* pools of gushy, goopy, glorious mud can entertain children of all ages for hours at a time. That is, until last week, when a little boy down the street reminded me what excitement awaits those who take the time to go outside and play in the mud. I should probably mention that "the little boy down the street" is six feet tall, and a grandfather of seven.

First, let me set the stage before I give you the scoop on this story. Our family lives on the banks of a small lake, in a neighborhood of about a hundred cabins that dot the surrounding woods. Living near water has been an adventure in and of itself, but one of the most interesting events in our neighborhood happens when the board members of our community decide it is time to drain the lake—for dock repairs, or to plant fish-attracting algae or, I suspect, simply to satisfy curiosities about what's lurking under the water. One thing is certain: The best thing lurking is mud; the thickest, goopiest, doggone best mud a young boy or old man could ever hope to squish-squash around in.

Our kids—from nine-year-old Gabriel on up to sixteen-year-old Zach—have invented a new sport of their own to play during these times of forced lake drought. Although, temporarily, there is no boating, skiing, fishing, or swimming, our children are far from depressed when the water is drained. They now have—muddin'. "What's muddin'?" you ask. Perhaps I should simply explain how muddin' is carried out, and I think you'll get the general idea.

To get the most from the muddin' experience, you first pull on the tallest pair of rubber boots you can find—hip boots are best. Then, starting from the shore, the object of the game is to wade toward the middle of what used to be the lake, venturing out and in as deep as you dare. Our teenagers routinely make it clear up to their necks in black goop. And that's about the gist of it.

"Why would anyone in his or her right mind want to do this?" you may ask. I don't know; believe me, I don't know. I was a child of more dainty constitution, myself. But my kids absolutely love this activity, and since muddin' keeps them happy and busy and out of my hair—and since I suppose it's an invigorating form of isometric exercise—I hold my tongue. As long as they spray off with the hose in the yard before setting a toe on my carpet, I'm pretty easygoing about such things.

I inherited this attitude, I think, from my own mother. She never blinked about letting us kids play outside in the rain. In reference to such leniencies (or lunacies, as the case may be), one of my boys once complimented me by saying, "Mom, I'm so glad you aren't sensible like other mothers." "Thank your Granny," I said.

There is one thing I protest about the muddin' days, however. Every now and then, one of my children will dig up and bring into the house a horrible, vile-looking, hissing eel-like creature—about a foot long and an inch and a half thick. They find them burrowing into the mud along the banks. The critters go by the name of "mud puppies" around here, much too sweet a name for these miniature horror monsters if you ask me. They give me the heebie-jeebies and look just like offspring of those blood-sucking earth-eels from the movie *Tremors.*

Once Gabriel brought a mud puppy into the bathroom and left it unattended in some tap water in the sink. I didn't realize it was there, came along, and reached into the sink to the plug. Before that fat eel disappeared down the drain like slick fettuccine, he managed to slither around my hand just to let me know he was there. As you might expect, I screamed until there were no screams left in me. Now I have a *permanent* case of the heebie-jeebies. I keep expecting that someday a slimy black creature will return and pop its hissing head up out of the sink, just when I least expect it. And I will simply die. That's all. I'll just die.

Now back to the little boy/grandfather. His name is Wally. Wally decided the other morning that it would be a great idea, while the water was down, to dig some deep pools around the edge of the lake—pools where fish could eventually congregate so fishermen could eventually do the same. In truth, I strongly suspect Wally simply had a hankering to dig a big hole with a great big tractor. And so, when his wife went shopping and promised to be gone for the entire morning, Wally set out to go play in the mud with his man-sized Tonka truck.

In our neighborhood, the sound of a tractor or backhoe's engine is like the call of a roaring pied piper to every machine-loving male within hearing distance. So it wasn't long before Wally had a crowd of playmates around him, eager to help, or at least to provide him with an audience. It goes without saying that as soon as the sound of a heavy-duty engine drifted through the back door, Scott walked outside toward the noise like some beguiled sleepwalker in a cartoon—not blinking, not uttering a word. On his hypnotic trek toward the big-machine noise, Scott ran into Jim Ed, our no-nonsense, laid-back neighbor.

"Hey, Jim Ed!" Scott called, "What's goin' on down there by the lake?"

"Wally thinks he's going to dig himself a fishin' hole," Jim Ed replied. "I tried to tell him it was still too muddy."

"So what are you going to do now?" Scott asked.

"Well," drawled Jim Ed, "guess I'll pour me a cup of coffee and come sit out here on the porch. Then I think I'll watch a tractor sink."

Jim Ed's not only no-nonsense and laid-back—he's smart. He sat down just in time to see Wally drive the tractor six feet out from the edge of the mud and watch it sink nearly six feet under. Talk about your mud on your face. Wally was in it at least up to his hip boots, and Scott walked back in the house to give an updated blow-by-blow report.

"Becky," he informed me, "Wally's going to have to rent a big diesel truck to come pull that tractor out. Can you believe it?" I could tell my husband was working hard at trying to disguise the little-boy excitement that kept trying to creep into his manly, serious voice.

"Honey," I answered brightly, "I think it is just wonderful of Wally to do this on a holiday, so all you neighborhood guys can be in on this while you've got time off to enjoy it. You couldn't pay for a better male-bonding experience than this—men, mud, big tractors, trucks. Shall I make popcorn?"

"No time," Scott answered, no longer even attempting to hide his grin. "I gotta get back out there! Tell the boys to get out of bed; they'll want to see this!"

That evening I visited with Wally's wife. She was sitting on the couch, staring off into space, shaking her head back and forth, and mumbling. "Five hours," she said over and over again to herself. "I only left him alone for five hours. . . ." Bless her heart, we women are going to have to pull together, I can tell. Until that mud is covered up once again with lake, I'm afraid none of us can completely relax. All we can do is try to keep a better eye on our kids—large and small—while they play in the mud: goopy, squishy, gushy, glorious, eternally magnetic mud.

Post-Script: After reading this story and admitting to finding it a mite funny, Wally wrote me the following note. "I do want to set the record straight, however. WE DID GET ONE FISH-ING HOLE! When that big diesel truck upsurged the tractor, it left a pretty nice bass hole. Not a big one and we don't want to estimate dollars per cubic feet—but it will provide a home for several lake bass." Consider the record straightened!

God, save me. The water has risen to my neck.
I'm sinking down into the mud. There is
nothing to stand on. I am in deep water.
PSALM 69:1–2, NCV

Can I Hug the Bunny?

During their third-grade year at school, each of my children colored and cut out a large paper-doll-sized boy and named him "Flat Stanley." Then, along with all the kids in their class, they mailed Flat Stanley to an adult friend or relative to take on an "adventure." The adult was then to take the "paper boy" along for the day, write about what they did together, take pictures if possible, and mail him back to the child's school for "show and tell."

This year, Gabe had his turn at making a Flat Stanley. But then Gabe was faced with a dilemma. Who on earth could he trust to be an adventurous companion for his paper boy? Only one person, Gabe realized, might be up for the task. It had to be someone who knew how to handle a camera. It had to be someone with a vivid imagination. It had to be someone who still liked kid stuff. It had to be Grandma.

I don't know much about the childhood of Gabe's paternal grandmother, Beverly. Oh, here and there she's shared some scattered memories of sunny days growing up in California. But I've had the feeling that Bev's childhood went by way too fast for her liking. Like a piece of gum one is forced to spit out too soon, childhood often disappears before we have a chance to chew all the "goody" out of it.

So, over the last few years, I've been casually observing my mother-in-law as she paints more "childlikeness" into her adult days—using colors of her own whim and fancy. I, for one, think it's marvelous.

One childlike, fun thing Bev has started doing over the past few years is collecting teddy bears. This Christmas, we gave her a tapestry teddy and a teddy bear wreath. Other grown children and grandchildren gifted her with a leather-attired motorcycle bear and a ready-for-the-slopes snow ski bear. Bev's now acquired more than fifty-seven bears—enough to decorate a Christmas tree from top to bottom. Though it is now the end of February, the Bear Tree is still up, and I have a sneaking suspicion it is not coming down anytime soon. The nice thing about getting old is that you can eat dessert first and keep a Christmas tree up until July if you jolly well please.

And so it followed quite naturally that when Flat Stanley arrived in Grandma's mailbox, she'd choose to take him along on an adventure with her bear friends. The result was not just a quick letter and a handful of pictures. Oh, no. Grandma wrote and photographed an entire book about Flat Stanley's adventures. Flat Stanley on the Bear Tree. Flat Stanley sailing in a basket with the Quadruplet Sailor Bears. Flat Stanley on Grandpa's motorcycle with Motorcycle Bear. Flat Stanley cooking beans with Chef Bear. Gabe was delighted.

As I read through Beverly's wondrous book, I thought of a passage I'd read recently about mid-life choices. Paula Payne Hardin has a chapter called "The Child of Yesterday, The Adult of Today" in her book, *What Are You Going to Do with the Rest of Your Life?*

"One day," she writes, "I realized I wanted to go to a toy store and find a teddy bear. This may appear foolish to some—a woman in her fifties wanting a teddy bear, but it was my desire. I found a wonderful furry creature who called out to me from his deep-set brown yes. I was so excited!" She even wrote a sonnet of her experience called "In Praise of Teddy Bears." In the sonnet she expressed how her bear comforted her with its soft, accepting presence. "So grown-ups, hug your bears with heart's delight!"[15] the sonnet encourages.

"Come on," I'm sure some calloused soul out there is protesting. "We're talkin' about a stuffed piece of fluff!" My answer to this logical argument is, "Never underestimate the power of fluff."

Even my upper-level business executive father still keeps his old, pitiful, adorable, gray stuffed elephant in the top of his closet. The fur has mostly been rubbed off. One of its button eyes is—sorry to say this, Daddy—a socket of stuffing. But don't make fun of this stuffed baby elephant around my father. He transforms instantly into a boy of about five. "That was my Dumbo," he softly reminisces. And I can almost visualize a hazy image of my daddy as a little boy going off to sleep with his arms around his baby elephant.

On my trip to Disneyland, I bought a brand new stuffed Dumbo and mailed it off to my father. I wasn't back home in Texas for long before my parents showed up for a visit. When I opened the front door, there stood my dad, stroking the velvet pink ears of his new baby elephant toy. In his classic "little boy" voice he said, "I like my Dumbo." Mother shook her head in mock worry.

"Becky," she said, "he's been under so much stress at work lately, I'm a little worried he's going to take that elephant into a board meeting."

When Scott was young, he had a stuffed monkey. He also had an imaginary friend named Joe, who lived in the closet. When Scott talks of Joe and his monkey, his voice also slides back in time until he's sounding like a small boy. Funny how people do that. Everyone I ask about their special childhood companion begins to revert, without thinking, to using baby talk as they describe their treasured friend.

———

As an adult, my husband continues to keep friendly stuffed animals around. But now, the more macho name for them is "his truck mascots." He has a soft, squishy, stuffed cow with long spindly legs. Ingeniously, he named her "Cow." Recently, he added a stuffed moose to the front-seat menagerie. You guessed it. "Moose."

My children have also had their assorted stuffed "friends." Zach took lots of teasing over it, but when he was a little tike he toted around a "Buddy"—a stuffed boy dressed in overalls and a cap. Zeke had a fluff-and-battery-filled Glo-Worm that lit up the dark night. He called it his Glo-Buggy. Scott and I secretly called it his Bed Bug. Rachel, at age twelve, is completely enamored with her stuffed Pooh Bear. We even had a Winnie the Pooh birthday party for her this year. I'm amused to see toddler toys are "in" with teens right now. Have you noticed? In the malls more and more teenagers are sporting Piglet watches, Mickey Mouse shirts, and Tweety Bird ball caps. It sure beats satanic rock group attire all to pieces, I say.

Gabe has Big Bear, a huge, floppy, huggable bear, three feet tall and three feet wide. Even when Gabe was only three feet tall himself, he'd insist on taking Big Bear everywhere. (I even let him take Big Bear to the grocery store with us. Where, I now wonder, did I ever put the groceries? Desperate moms will find a way to put up with *anything* if it keeps their preschoolers quiet on shopping trips.) Seven years later, Big Bear still occupies one-fourth of Gabe's bed. Says he still loves his bear and "will never ever get rid of him."

This Valentine's Day, Gabe wanted to give his little girlfriend the best present his savings could buy. So he gathered up all his dollars, quarters, dimes, and pennies and bought her the biggest, softest, fluffiest, white teddy bear he could find. She loved it and told him so. He was so touched he wrote her the following note, which I found on my computer.

> I'm glad you liked you'r teddeybear. I rote a rime
> for you it goe'es like this I think you'r grandey I

think you'r handey & I like to give canddey. I
know it's short but you know I love you & that's all
that matter's. love, Gabe

(They also had to write what they liked most about Valentine's Day. I got a kick out of his paper.)

I'm polst to tell you good things about Valen-
tims. They are giving presents becouse it's fun to
watch them open it. I usually give my friends stufft
bears & chocklets. The party's are fun becouse we
get cookies, candy, Sprite, & I can be with my
friends. I just flat out like Vallintines.

(I can't help myself. It's hard not to smile when you've got a
frog-loving, bear-hugging kid around the house.)

As my sweet grandmother, Nonnie, moved into her eighties,
someone gave her a pretty, soft doll with flaxen hair and a pink
folk-style dress. Nonnie named the doll Ursula and kept her
primped and propped on her bed. Grandchildren and great-
grandchildren could freely play with anything in Nonnie's
house, but it always made her nervous if little grubby fingers got
too close to her Ursula.

One day Nonnie had a stroke and had to enter the cold stark-
ness of a hospital. Ursula came along too. I remember Mother
commenting on how bittersweet it was to see her aging mother
comforted, in strange antiseptic surroundings, by the presence of
a familiar doll.

What about me? Well, I never had a special stuffed piece of
lovable fluff as a child. I had a doll that I loved, but no soft bear
or monkey or elephant that stole my heart. As I was writing this
chapter, I realized this made me a little sad. Then one day I was
in a toy store, around Easter, and I picked up a stuffed bunny
with big floppy ears and huge feet with calico pads. And it fit
perfectly in my arms.

So, at age thirty-seven, I marched up to the counter and
bought myself a bunny. I took him home, put him on my bed—

and I absolutely love him. It's become a sweet family joke. When one of the kids is sick or needs some TLC, they'll pitifully moan, "Mom, can I borrow your bunny?" Scott came home once after an especially grueling day, stretched out on the bed, and stared at the ceiling. When I asked him what I could do to help, he gruffly replied, "Bring me that bunny."

This very afternoon I met a precious woman who often hosts women's retreats in her log home. She also collects teddy bears. "Becky," she said, "one time I was preparing for the ladies to come, and I felt the Lord wanted me to give away three of my bears. So I set them aside, thinking to myself, *Oh, they are going to think this is so silly.* But during a sharing time, three of the women shared heartbreaking stories of childhood abuse. Then I told them what God had impressed upon me earlier and handed each woman a bear, saying, 'God wants you to enjoy your childhood starting *now.*' They couldn't say anything. They just hugged those bears and bawled. It was beautiful."

Every grown-up who has ever been a child—or is part child still—understands that there is more to bunnies and bears and monkeys than fluff and stuff. In a popular story about a little boy who was afraid of the dark, the mother tells her son that he can rest assured that God is always with him, even in the night.

"Yes," the little boy answers, "but I need somebody with skin on." And in the absence of "somebody with skin on," I believe the next best thing to snuggle up with in the dark is something soft and fluffy—with fur on.

The poor man had nothing except one little ewe lamb he had bought. . . . It grew up with him and his children. It . . . slept in his arms.

2 SAMUEL 12:3

❧

But I Don't Wanna
Go Home Yet!

I am bummed. I mean, I'm *really* bummed out. I just got home from summer vacation, you see, and I'm not quite ready for life. It's like I found the most perfect, peaceful place to hide. Then just as I settled into a calm "ahhh . . .," big, clumsy ol' Real Life shouts, "Ready or not, here I come!" And within seconds, I am discovered and hauled by the scruff of my neck into the game against my will.

This morning, life forced me up early and into a game of Follow the Kids to the Station Wagon. Upon my offspring's arrival at the car doors, all four of them broke out in a rousing chorus of "I Get the Front Seat." The participants then began to battle each other in what looked like a wild game of Twister—all tangled up trying to reach the coveted seat of honor. At that point I changed the game to Let's Make a Deal, claimed Monopoly on the front seat, and refused to move until all children were ready to participate in Sorry. (OK, enough of the game motif.)

After finally depositing the children at school, I drove back home, and it was then I realized the horrible truth. Today, all by myself, I'd have to clean the whole entire yucky house; cook supper—from scratch, mind you—and *then* make wild after-school zigzags all over town picking up my umpteen kids from every conceivable form of "practice." Not only that, but I'd also have to sit down and work, which means actually *using my brain* to make sense of the little black marks floating across the computer screen at the tap of my fingers. Am I starting to sound just a wee bit ugly? Forgive me, but sometimes I get so frustrated. Can you indulge my tantrum just a second longer?

Here's the news that really rots my sandals: Waiting to greet me on my office desk is IRS Form 1040A—the incredibly, unbelievably looooong version, along with all of its tricky little friends—8898, 4562, and Schedules A-Z. (Yes, I should have filed them in April, but I always file for the extension. Never do today what you can put off for four months, I always say.)

As a result, I'm cross-eyed and bewildered and, yes, even para-noid. I just know there is an IRS agent with beady little eyes and an evil sense of humor sitting in some government office waiting for me to misplace a decimal. (Um, just in case an IRS agent is reading this—I'm just teasing with the "beady little eyes, evil sense of humor" bit. But according to line 42, section b, page 55-A—I believe "teasing about the IRS" is "allowable.")

I want you to know that all of this nonproductive whining does have a point—*but what was it?* Oh, yes. The transition from play time to clean-up time is the *pits*. I hated it in kinder-garten, and I don't like it any better as an adult. Visualize a tod-dler wailing—one of those open-mouthed, out-loud whines—and you'll have a perfect picture of how I feel right now.

I don't wanna go home yet! I'll do my chores next month! I wanna go back and play some more!! WAAAAAH!!!

But maybe [sniff, sniff] if I could tell you how much fun I had on my summer vacation [pitiful swallow], and about the good time I had with my friends, maybe I'll feel all better again.

First and foremost, I've got to tell you about the great big ocean. (Hang on to your visors; I'm about to wax poetic.)

I could sit for hours near the sea, watching her emerald waves toss up soft foam toward sandy shores, then pull it all back out again—as if reluctant to hand over such lacy treasure. Show and tell, take it back, then show and tell again.

The beach is also a rather noisy place. Yet the noise of the waves is another thing I love about retreating to the sea. I don't believe people usually come to the ocean to *sort through* complicated problems. The din of sloshing sea water assures active thinking will be kept to a minimum, at best. I believe, instead, that people come to the ocean to be *swept away*—to let the crashing, repetitive sound of the pounding waves wash out tired, muddled heads. The laborious swooooosh . . . swooooosh . . . swooooosh . . . leaves you empty, limp, and clean. Like a head massage. Or a mental rinse. I guess you could say it's a lovely experience in brainwashing. And the sheer gift of a nonthinking day spent watching the gentle tug of war between sea and shore, and of listening to the white noise of the playful struggle—well, that's only the *beginning.*

It is at night, after the sun makes its crimson bow, all glitter comes out for display. On this particular trip, a full moon dropped by for a welcome visit. I'd never seen a full moon over the ocean at night, and I almost ached with the beauty of the thing. Luminescent, with its eye wide open, hovering over the dark velvet waves—like something wise, gentle, maternal. In response to the glowing roundness in the sky, thousands of diamond lights danced their gratitude from tops of rolling sea water.

Walking over a dune that night, unprepared as I was for the gorgeous panorama rising before my eyes, I understood the old expression, "It takes my breath away." When I found my breath, I whispered quiet praise to the Artist of the masterpiece.

Isn't this a good vacation story so far? My brow is already beginning to unfurrow. By the time I'm finished recounting

"My Summer Vacation," I may even feel some measure of warmth toward the IRS.

Right about now I suppose you might be asking, "Just exactly what did you do on vacation besides participate in poetic waxing?" OK, OK, I'm getting to that. I did absolutely anything I wanted to do at any given moment. For days—six of them to be exact.

Actually, I did do *some* things. I made our bed once or twice, but I must confess—I enjoyed it. Even housework can be fun in tasteful surroundings belonging to wealthy, yuppy-condo-landlords. The furniture in our bedroom was white wicker, the walls pale green, the bedspread thick and covered with fat pink roses. And there was a lovely balcony where I could slip out at any time to rest between the exertion of fluffing pillows and tucking in coverlets.

I also did a little cooking—toast, salad, and cold cereal. Seriously, I did manage to whip up some real live meals. There are witnesses that can testify that I also made chili dogs, Bisquick biscuits, and coleslaw from a mix. Somehow, we managed to eat well.

One of the best parts of our annual vacation is that we always go with two sets of old friends—Ron and Gail, and Dean and Heather—and their children. Luckily, Gail can cook—rich treats like pecan brownies and sour cream coffee cake—from *scratch*. And Heather—well, Heather knows how to both buy and boil shrimp. And because she's got just the right touch of obsessive-compulsiveness, the kitchen stays spotless. Culinary matters aren't of much consequence anyway, since eating out at oceanside cafés has become our group's favorite all-weather water sport.

When vacationing with others, we've found it's important to have similar likes and dislikes. For example, Gail and I are always on a budget, which we don't like. But then there's shopping—which we do like. Very much. Luckily, for determined bargain hunters like Gail and me—with little to no sense of pride—there's always a way to get our shopping fix. You should see the great stuff we've picked up from resale shops, Goodwill, and Salvation Army stores along the coastal highways!

One of our "finds" on this trip was a used bookstore. This particular bookstore was in a converted upstairs apartment. It seemed odd that the young proprietor was wearing a tie with his shirt, but he had recently retired from military service. He greeted us warmly and apologized for the mess, not knowing how really low our standards of neatness are. Since I read at least five books during vacation week, I love browsing for reading treasure—especially something that will touch my heart or lift my spirit. In the stacks of dusty books lining the floors and shelves, I found a couple of pearls: a fifty-year-old copy of *The Robe*, by Lloyd C. Douglas, and a thirty-year-old copy of *Gifts from the Sea*, by Anne Morrow Lindbergh.

When it was time to pay for our books, the military-type shopkeeper surprised us with a serendipitous method for determining the price. Flashing a smile, he asked, "Do you know the game 'Paper, Rock, Scissors'?" Puzzled, we nodded. "Well, here's the deal: If *you* win, you can name the price. But if *I* win, I get to set the price." He continued, "Fair enough?"

We were game. Why not? Unfortunately, Bookstore Man won. I held my breath, waiting to hear his price.

"How does two dollars sound?" he asked. *For two hardback books? Are you kidding?* I thought. He charged Gail an entire $1.50 for her small stack.

As we turned to leave with our bargains, already tickled with our good fortune, our young man pulled fresh flowers from a nearby vase and handed each of us one as a parting gift. We felt like school girls.

A surprising number of the people we met in Florida went out of their way to be pleasant. Maybe it's the climate. Maybe it's the simple way of life—shorts and sandals are standard attire in even the finest of restaurants. Perhaps it's just that people in Florida stay in an eternally pleasant state of mind. We even came upon a nearby town called Niceville. *Niceville?* Gail and I had to check it out. We found a native Nicevillian working behind a convenience store counter and plied him with all sorts of questions.

"Are people really *nice* here? Is there always a breeze? Do you ever see mosquitoes? What are the schools like? How's the crime rate? Do you just *love* living here?"

I never thought I'd ever consider moving from our East Texas home, but I was tempted for the first time in years to pull up anchor and move to the oceanside.

If Gail keeps me company on shopping sprees, then Heather's my comrade in devouring books and also in the quest to know the answer to everything there is to know about everything—especially about the true meaning of life. One night, the rest of the clan went out for a while, leaving us bookworms alone in the living room. But as soon as the door slammed shut, Heather sat up with a start, put her book down, and fired her opening sentence.

"OK, Becky, let's catch up!"

And we were off! At the end of an hour, we'd only hit the tip of our theological/philosophical icebergs. But just as we were getting warmed up, kids of all ages began pouring through the front door eager to share their latest adventure, and our time was gone.

Yes, it was a good vacation. Good friends, good conversation, good shopping, good food, *great* schedule.

And this year we also had lots of teenagers among the children in our group—our Zach, Zeke, and Rachel; Dean and Heather's nineteen-year-old, Jarin; and Ron and Gail's girls, Mandie-Lee, Laressa, and their friend, Amy. I must admit that much of my luxurious sense of freedom was because my children are entering a wonderful stage of independence. Those long years of having to be constantly on the lookout for little ones is fast coming to a close. (A wonderful consolation prize for failing my pregnancy test at the outset of this book!)

Our teens were amazingly uncomplaining, polite, fun, and just plain *good* this year, if I do say so myself. After watching them together this summer, I'm convinced they'll be friends for life. Just as we, their parents, have been all these years.

As an added bonus, a couple of our teenagers now drive. However, the only vehicle that would hold them all for their short excursions about town was poor old Sag. One year, within three hours of the resort, Sag suddenly expired on the highway. But after about ten minutes rest, he gathered up the strength to start his engine again and mosied on down the highway for another hour, whereupon he felt the need for another roadside break. At the time, none of Sag's weary contents found this amusing. But a couple of days after we'd said our "good-byes" to the beach and unpacked our bags in Texas, I found a letter in the mailbox addressed to "Sag & Those Within." It said,

Dear Sag, We wrote this in your honor.
Thanks for the memories.

Sag, the Tragic Wagon
Traveled to the sea
And weaved all over I–20
As far as we could see

Sag, the Tragic Wagon
Had traveled there before
But previously had to stop and rest
Every hour, and sometimes more!

Sag, the Tragic Wagon
Had many squished in the back
Including one lonely watermelon,
Gabe, Zeke, Rach-el, and Zach!

Love,
Mandie-Lee, Laressa, and Amy

Is this not *moving?* Brings tears to a mother's eyes. The ocean has now even inspired our children to wax poetic!

———

Well, that's pretty much the end of my summer vacation story. Wow. I feel so much better. I really do. Thanks for hearing me out. I think I may have the strength to tackle ol' 1040 and 8898 now.

Wait a second. One last thought. Since vacation did me such a world of good, I wonder if people who may be thinking about checking into a mental hospital ought to try "six days of doing nothing at the beach" first. It would be much less expensive over the long haul, a lot more fun, and honestly, what harm can it do? After all, if you're still nuts at the end of six days, the mental ward will always be there.

I know one thing for sure; every chance I get I plan to do more Nothing. As that wise old philosopher, Winnie the Pooh, once said, "Don't underestimate the value of Doing Nothing, of just going along, listening to all the things you can't hear, and not bothering." If I do not take periodic getaways, I'm afraid life will leave me playing "Ring Around the Rosie" at some loony farm way before my time. And I need my faculties in working order so I can enjoy the golden years with Dean and Heather and Ron and Gail in our Florida retirement villa—where we'll play in God's giant sandbox all day and watch the moon pour over His wave pool at night. (How long does it take to reach those golden years anyway?)

Hey, since you've been such a great help to me today, please feel free to call us in about twenty-five years and drop by for the fun. I'll even make chili dogs and Bisquick biscuits and coleslaw for supper. And it goes without saying, you'll find us listed in the Niceville directory.

> *"Come to me, all you who are weary and*
> *burdened, and I will give you rest."*
> MATTHEW 11:28

ॐ

Old People Can Make Pretty Good Kids

I met a kid yesterday at a local folk festival. He was having an absolute ball playing around with a couple of sticks—in front of anybody who'd pause long enough to watch the show. So I asked this kid, "How old are you anyway?"

"I turned seventy this year," he answered with a grin.

This gentleman was one of *several* lively senior citizens Scott and I met yesterday. They didn't appear to be ready for retirement homes, although several seemed likely candidates for kindergarten—especially a kindergarten that allowed for plenty of play time. Now I'm *really* ready for retirement!

The "stick kid's" real name turned out to be Donald De Camp, but he goes by the name of "Mr. Bones." This was evident because the word *Bones* was engraved on the back of his leather belt. (Leather belts substitute for business cards and billboards among folk festival types.) He goes by "Mr. Bones" because he *plays* the bones. Not the ones attached to his skeleton, but two pieces of bird's-eye maple carved into the shape and size of a couple of thick bookmarks.

Held loosely between the fingers, they snap out infinite and complicated rhythms to the harmonies of guitars, banjos, dulcimers, and such. Mr. Bones played his sticks two sets at a time—a pair going in each hand. I must say it was an awe-inspiring sight for all who watched this performer at work.

Scott and I took advantage of an opportunity to visit with Bones during a break. As the old gentleman wiped the sweat from his forehead, he said, "Man, oh man. I *love* that rhythm!" Now he wasn't referring to a particular rhythm in a particular song. He loved the big idea of rhythm, the entire *concept* of rhythm, any regular beat that allowed him the chance to get out his sticks and go play.

He told us that years ago the "bones" were originally made from animal bones. He'd even found some evidence that the bones, as musical instruments, had been in existence some 1,500 years before Christ. Young Donald De Camp had picked them up as a child for the pure fun of it and has been playing them ever since. That's all the information we could squeeze out of our conversation, because the band started again and all his friends began begging him to come out and play with them some more. He bowed his apologies to us young'uns, shuffled to center stage, closed his eyes for a moment, then went to tapping and dancing and playing those bones. He was wild joy on the loose.

Scott's eyes followed Bones' every movement—my husband has always been an admirer of old codgers, especially the sort with plenty of twinkles left in their eyes.

I imagine if Scott were to write a male version of the famous poem, "When I Am Old I Shall Wear Purple," it might go something like this:

> When I am old, I shall wear my hair in tufts of
> sweepy silver 'round the perimeter of my
> head.

I shall wear old boots and faded jeans and a
tanned leather belt with my name on the
back.
I shall own a crisp white shirt, a black string tie,
a handsome vest and a pocket watch, with a
gold chain that loops in front.
I shall close my eyes when I hear the band start
up and I shall wander toward
the sounds until the beat collides with the joy in
my heart.
And I shall dance.
Alone, or with a pretty gal, or with my best set
of bones.
And I shall make all the young ones wish they
were old—
old enough to shuffle centerstage and play
with the abandon of an uninhibited soul.

Sometime after our encounter with Bones, we heard the sound of a soulful tenor drifting above the crowd. It was accompanied by an instrument that sounded something like the warble of a bird or a woman's voice. Following the beautiful strains, we came upon a most unlikely sight. A rather dapper looking gentleman (even though clad in overalls) was sitting and playing a handsaw. He held the handsaw tucked under one thigh and ran a violin's bow across the smooth side of the blade, producing an almost other-worldly melody.

This unusual musician was also the source of the incredible tenor voice. Many of us in the crowd stood misty-eyed, listening to that voice tenderly pour the words to "Danny Boy" from his soul to ours. Only a true Irishman could evoke the sort of emotion this man pulled from the small audience around him. He finished up the last strains a cappella, ending the final notes with a gallant sweeping of the black derby from his head and over his heart.

We gave the Irishman our compliments during a break and discovered he went by the name of Ramblin' Ray Rickets. He hailed from Arkansas, so his Southern accent left no hint of an Irish brogue. But, sure 'n' sure, he was Irish of soul. Said he could sing "Danny Boy" every day of his life and never grow tired of it.

As we had done with Mr. Bones, we asked Ray how he came to play his unusual instrument. He smiled and smoothed back his hair with his hand before replacing the derby atop its silvery perch.

"It was real simple. I heard our preacher play the saw one Sunday in our li'l ol' country church, and I went up right after the service and asked him if he'd show me how to do it. Right then and there, the preacher sat down and gave me a quick lesson—and I was hooked. Took it right up and never put it down."

I could see Scott making a mental list—a list I knew he'd eventually bring to a hardware store: bird's-eye maple, new handsaw, violin bow. Later in the afternoon, we passed table after table of wood carvings, and visited with elderly craftsmen as they carved their works of butternut, maple, and other delicious-sounding woods. These men, too, were a friendly, most contented looking lot. Scott added "a porch swing, butternut, and a whittlin' knife" to his growing list of necessities. (He plans to get a running start on ol' codgerdom.)

Watching all the fiddlin' and whittlin' and cloggin' and sawin' made us suddenly aware we were hungry. Two dishes of homemade vanilla ice cream hit the spot and satisfied our hunger. Well, almost. Of course, there was no way I could pass the funnel cake booth—with its swirls of fried bread piled high with fresh whipped cream and juicy strawberries.

Moments later, Scott instructed me to wipe the bits of berries and cream off my face, then asked me to dance a couple of impromptu waltzes and a schottische with him—right there on the street. After all, we'd just seen ol' Bones take off with his sweetheart and twirl her around to a western swing. We couldn't let the old folk beat us completely into the ground. Scott and I were getting more childlike and frisky by the minute. Being around happy, unrestrained people over the age of sixty was beginning to have a youthful effect on us.

As the sun began to fade and the autumn air cooled, we found ourselves wandering back in the direction of our Irish friend. As we'd hoped, Ray was still happily "sawing" away. The crowds were gone, so Scott and I sat down, propped our feet up on empty chairs, and listened to the music serenade the nightfall. A younger man on Ray's left was doing a fine job of picking his banjo, a woman to his right was belting out an old mournful ballad as she strummed her guitar. After a couple of melancholy tunes, Ray looked up at us and winked.

"These old songs are so sad, it's a wonder we're not all depressed."

I laughed and said, "It's OK. Just sing us a 'hallelujah' song in between the depressin' ones now and then."

"I'd like to do you one better than that, right after we finish this next heartbreaker."

Scott put his arm around me and stroked my shoulder as we waited, peacefully, for our love-graced day to come gently to its end. The group sang their last sad song for my husband and me, their only audience. No matter. These artists performed for the simple pleasure of sending their music into the air. Finally, the young banjo player set his instrument down, looked at the woman, at Ray, at us.

"Now this has been what I call a *festival*," he declared.

Scott and I rose to give the group a two-person standing ovation, but Ray asked us to sit for just a minute longer.

"I'd like to say an Irish blessing for you two."

With that, he stood, swept the derby from his head, and placed it over his heart once more, pronouncing a benediction befitting the day.

"May the road rise up to meet you, may the sun shine warm upon your face, the rains fall soft upon your fields, and, until we meet again, may God hold you in the palm of His hand."

What a wonderful thing it was to be blessed in such a way. How precious, how rare.

"Thank you so much," I said, standing to leave with Scott. "You've made our day."

Scott nodded in agreement. "Yes, it's been an honor."

"No," Ray leaned a little on his saw, placed one knee up on a chair, and argued, "*you* have honored *us*."

It's not easy to find childlike fun and thoughtfulness in and among human beings these days. Yet all in one day we were privileged to witness those very qualities in several fine people—the likes of Bones and Ramblin' Ray.

Victor Hugo once said, "Winter is on my head, but eternal spring is in my heart." Or as my eternally young mother puts it, West Texas–style, "Just 'cause thar's a little snow on the roof, don't mean there ain't a fire in the furnace."

They will still bear fruit in old age, they will
stay fresh and green.
PSALM 92:14

TWENTY-EIGHT

Hey, I've Got a Great Idea!

Seeing a book nearing its end is a little like watching a first child go off to kindergarten (especially, this *particular* book). The ending of an era is always fraught with ambiguity. On one hand, I'm ready to let 'er rip, fling this prose out the door, and get on with life! On the other hand, I worry there might be just one more thing I need to say before completely letting go. I've only just begun to scratch the surface on the benefits of behaving like a child! Inevitably, as soon as my manuscript is cuddled, bundled, kissed good-bye and deposited at the post office, I'll remember another story or think of one more piece of advice that would have been "just perfect" for the book—if only I could climb into that little mailbox slot and retrieve the package.

But I must begin to let go, for my sake and the sake of my family. The other day Scott drove our family through Burger King (the drive-thru, not the building) and placed an order for french fries. He also asked for some ketchup, and on reflex, I found myself bouncing up and down in my seat chanting, "Ask for bunches and bunches and *bunches* of ketchup!" Like robots, my entire family stopped moving at once, slowly turning all heads and eyes on me. Finally, Scott spoke on behalf of the group.

"Becky, *where* did *that* come from?"

"Um," I replied sheepishly, "from the little girl inside me?"

"Becky, this childlike stuff is getting out of hand. You're acting so young you're embarrassing the *children*."

"Okeydokey," I said cheerfully, as I twirled my hair around my finger and stared wistfully out the window.

Perhaps I am getting a little carried away. But in my own defense, the idea of staying childlike into our adult years has been around for a very, very long time. Mencius from the third century B.C. wrote, "The great man is he who does not lose his child's-heart." I think ol' Mencius knew what he was talking about.

How do we turn our mid-life crisis into kid-life creativity? I have a great idea! How about starting a list, maybe even keeping it up on the refrigerator, of things we can do to help us find our child-heart when it wanders too far down Growing Up Lane. Here are a few suggestions to get you started, off the top of my wee little head.

Keep Asking Questions, Even If It Drives People Crazy

As you may have already guessed, Gabriel is—hands down— our family's top Weird Question Asker. A couple of weeks ago, he called me to the living room with an urgent, pertinent question: "Mom, what is that little dip called on top of your upper lip and under your nose?" I had to confess, once again, Gabe had me stumped. In my thirty-seven years, I can't say I'd ever, even once, given a thought to the dip above our lips. So I asked Scott to relay the question to a friend of ours, a physician.

"The medical term?" our doctor friend asked after Scott described the part of the body in question.

"Yep," Scott replied, "Gabe needs to know."

"Beats me," the good doctor replied. "But my best guess is that it's probably known as The Lip Dip."

It's questions like this that keep medical science on its toes—and the curiosity of a child alive in your heart.

Never Outgrow Children's Books

Just as children give us wonderful excuses to go see animated movies, they're also great reasons to reread favorite books from childhood (or discover new ones for your second go-around at kidhood).

I remember my third grade teacher as being pretty and young, but so, so sad. We found out later in the year that her husband had been killed in Vietnam just before she came to our school. The one bright spot of those melancholy classroom days was listening to her read from Laura Ingalls Wilder's *Little House in the Big Woods.*

During those fifteen minutes, while my teacher read aloud, I could escape the classroom for the hearthside of Pa and Ma Ingalls, Mary, Laura, and Baby Carrie. I'd feel cozy and happy and warm inside, as my mind drifted to the little log cabin in the big woods. Not surprisingly, this was the first "chapter book" I read to my own children, and I must admit I read it for my pleasure as much as for theirs.

Other classics I've loved and reread to children are: *The Box Car Children; Pippi Longstocking; Charlotte's Web; James and the Giant Peach; The Lion, the Witch, and the Wardrobe.* There are so many wonderful, *unforgettable* children's books worth reading with or without kids nearby, simply to keep a fresh, child's-eye view alive and well. Some of the most beautiful artwork anywhere can be had for the price of a children's book. I've collected about a hundred illustrated books. They're a treasure I can share with children now—and look forward to sharing with my grandbabies-to-be someday in the future. (Note to my teenage sons: in the far, far distant future.)

Don't Be Afraid to Be a Little Goofy

I have in my repertoire several examples of personal goofiness to choose from—as you might expect—but I'll narrow it down to one recent example. About a month ago, I had a flat tire. Well, it was more like a blowout—the steel belt had popped open but the tire still had air in it. When I drove the car forward, the belt made a horrendous sound as it flopped and slapped against raw metal. But when I drove it in reverse, the sound was much more subdued. So, to my children's horror and my neighbors' amazement, I drove all the way home in reverse. Five miles. All backwards. The funniest part was when we passed a poor, bewildered German shepherd. The pitiful thing really wanted to chase the car, but you could almost see him thinking, *Gee, which direction should I run?*

I must admit, I was not as embarrassed as most people might have been. There's a touch of little-kid mischief in me that enjoys keeping the neighborhood guessing about my sanity.

Be a Bubblegum Philosopher

As part of my journey to becoming a deeper thinking woman, I recently purchased a book written by Ravi Zacharias. In case, like me, you've been wading shallow intellectual waters the last few years and have not heard of him, Dr. Zacharias is a brilliant Christian philosopher who travels the world arguing for the existence of God in cerebral settings like Harvard and Princeton University.

I must confess, I've remained in a suspended state of insightful confusion throughout the first half of Dr. Zacharias's book, *Can Man Live without God?* Heavy reading is a lot like eating spinach: I know it's good for me, but hey, it's not chocolate cheesecake.

Then, just as my neurons refuse to stretch one more dendrite, Ravi breaks through with an easy-to-read story that even a kid like me can understand. Dr. Zacharias points out that G. K. Chesterton once "unabashedly proclaimed that he learned more about life by observing children in a nursery than he ever did by reflecting upon the writings of any of the philosophers."

This comforts me because I've been so busy changing diapers and wiping runny noses the last sixteen years I've had precious little time to delve into the great philosophies of the ages. Then Ravi proceeds to tell a remarkable story that points out exactly what I've been trying to explain for, lo, these many pages: There is a lot to be said for behaving like a child.

As the story goes, Ravi and his family were crossing from Jordan to Israel by way of the West Bank. Ushered into a highly secured immigration building to procure a visitor's visa, they had been warned to expect a long and grueling morning—in fact, the process might take all day. On every side, Dr. Zacharias, his wife, and his two-year-old daughter, Sarah, were surrounded by soldiers toting machine guns, "whose glares led us to believe that we were all guilty of something." From there, the scene Dr. Zacharias describes takes on an almost storybook quality.

> Finally it was our turn to be interrogated. Unknown to me, as she surveyed the room filled with armed guards, Sarah had locked eyes with a young Israeli soldier who was staring back at her in eye-to-eye "combat." Suddenly and strangely there was a moment of silence in the room, broken by the squeaky little voice of my daughter asking the soldier, "Excuse me, do you have any bubble gum?"
>
> Words alone cannot fully express to you what that little voice and plea did for everyone in the room, where hitherto the weapons of warfare and the world of "adult ideas" had held everyone at bay. All who understood English knew a soldier's heart had been irresistibly touched. All eyes were now on him.
>
> He paused for a moment, then carefully handed his machine gun to a colleague. He came over to where we were standing, looked endearingly at Sarah, and picked her up in his arms. He took her into a back room and returned a few minutes later with her in one arm, and in the other hand, he carried three glasses of lemonade on a tray—one for my wife, one for Sarah, and one for me. We were in and out of the immigration office in twenty-five minutes. In fact, the soldier brought his jeep to the door and drove us to the taxi stand, sending us on our way to Jericho.[16]

Leave it to a two-year-old to make lemonade out of machine guns—with bubblegum! So learn! Stretch! Grow intellectually! But don't forget to chew bubblegum while you're at it.

Be Aware of Guardian Angels

Cousin Jamie called the other day with a story about her youngest child, four-year-old Martha—a delicate, sweet, and shy little girl with soft blond hair and beautiful blue eyes and an adorable way of talking. Little Martha is even more precious to all of us after a recent close call.

Jamie and her mother (Martha's grandmother) had taken Jamie's four young children along on a shopping trip to a mall in Houston. When they were pooped out, they stopped to rest a moment near the bottom of an escalator. As kids will do, little Martha leaned her arms over the escalator's handrail, as she stood on the floor beside it watching people going up, up, up.

And as the railing also rose, Martha lifted her feet off the ground for a ride and before anyone knew what was happening, her small body began rising above the mall floor. She was dangling only by her tiny arms clinging to the escalator handrail. It all happened so fast that by the time Jamie looked up, screamed, and began sprinting up the steps to help her daughter, it was too late. When little Martha reached the top—twenty feet above the ground—she also hit the wall. Her grandmother watched in helpless horror as she saw one little hand let go and then the other.

And that's when the angels took over. A woman standing below the escalator happened to see what was going on, positioned herself, said a silent prayer for strength, and opened her arms. As Martha fell from the full height of twenty feet above the mall's tile floor, the woman made a successful catch. Both woman and child went down with the impact, but thankfully, both were unhurt. Of course, they were stunned.

Martha lay there in the woman's lap on the floor, perfectly still, not saying a word. Nothing seemed hurt, but she might have been in shock. After a long while, she wriggled and tugged at her rescuer's shirt. The woman leaned down closer to hear the quiet little voice. In the midst of noise and turmoil and Jamie's crying and the grandmother's sighs of relief, Martha had one concern on her ladylike four-year-old mind.

"My unduhweauh is showing," she whispered.

Jesus said, "Beware that you don't look down upon a single one of these little children. For I tell you that in heaven their angels have constant access to my Father" (Matt. 18:10, TLB). That's why the child in me *has* to believe that somewhere, watching over a Houston mall, unseen to the naked eye, a couple of guardian angels gave each other a high five and laughed a hearty chuckle.

This list could go on forever! I've not even touched on coloring with crayons, watching clouds float by, climbing a tree, eating popsicles, skimming stones across the pond, telling a knock-knock joke, running through a sprinkler, making up a silly song, decorating with wit and whimsy, going barefoot, or saying prayers like ,"I love You, Jesus. Amen"—and meaning it, and leaving it at that. The world is so full of simple, childlike joys. Why leave them behind when we can carry them with us?

It is no wonder we adults are stressed beyond reason. We've lost our child-heart! When was the last time you laid back in the grass, propped one foot over one knee, and made imaginary pictures out of clouds? Oh, the money we waste on spas and psychologists and pills, when time to meander and ponder and lay back in the grass is all most of us really need to get balanced again. I believe people today are *starving* for unscheduled blocks of precious time to *waste.* We know, instinctively, that our children need *time to be kids.*

But what about you? What about me?

My son just burst into my office, a baby turtle along for the ride in his grubby outstretched palm. He comes bearing important news. "Mom!" he says. "Remember that little seed that I planted? Well it plunked up from the dirt into leaves! Come see!" Now, should I keep writing or go outside with my child?

See ya later. I just made an appointment with a kid and some plunked-up leaves. Oh yes—and a sky full of clouds.

"I praise you, Father, Lord of heaven and earth,
because you have hidden these things
from the wise and learned,
and revealed them to little children."
MATTHEW 11:25

Look Daddy, I Can Fly!

Although I love the slinky, silky gowns my husband gives me every holiday season, this year I asked if he might give me something a little less breezy. I was particularly interested in sleepwear that would wrap warm and snugly around my cold, cold feet.

Thinking it would be a cute joke, Scott gave me a pair of "woman size" pink and white feety pajamas—in a teddy bear print. Christmas evening, I stole away to the bedroom and tried them on just for fun. As I put one foot and then another into the pajama legs, I drifted back to the very first memory I have as a child. I could almost hear my daddy—as he sounded nearly thirty-five years ago—softly singing, "Put your little foot, put your little foot, put your little foot right here. . . ." as I stood on my bed while he helped me into my feety pj's.

My father is one man who has managed, all his life, to keep his child-heart pumping strong.

One rainy spring afternoon, when I was about eleven, I went out in the garage to find my father ascending a ladder into the attic. Though Daddy was sentimental, he was *not* a handyman, so the sight of a ladder provoked my curiosity. Then he crooked his finger in a silent gesture that I knew meant, "Come along, but be quiet."

I followed him up into the attic and sat down beside him, curious as to the nature of our exploration. But all my dad said was, "Shhh . . . listen." Then I heard it. The rain, pattering over-head—amplified by our nearness to the rooftop.

"I come up here whenever it rains," Daddy said softly. It was cool and comforting, a tender moment caught—like a snap-shot—in my mind.

To my pleasant surprise, my husband turned out to be a rain-on-the-roof kind of guy, too. He even built our bed so that the head of it fits snug against a large picture window. At night, if the full moon is shining or a soft rain is falling, Scott pulls up the blinds and raises the window and whispers, "Shhh . . . Becky. Listen." And this, I believe, is part of the reason why the two men I love most in the whole world are my daddy and my hus-band.

Another thing I love about Daddy is the way he gave us kids silly nicknames. My little sister, Rachel, he nicknamed "The Bunky." Or sometimes he called her "Yupupuh." (Don't ask me where he got the inspiration for these.) When my brother, David, was small his word for "horses" came out as "saucies." Thus he earned the nickname "Saucy." When I was small, I wore a red ruffly nightgown, which I adored, and whenever I wore it Daddy called me his "Red Arriba." All of us kids collectively were dubbed "sproogins."

Another amazing thing about Daddy: In all my years, I cannot ever recall my father criticizing me. Not once. Always, he would praise and encourage my efforts—however crazy, how-ever childish.

Not long ago I had a dream; it is a reoccurring dream I've had for years. In it I can fly. I love these dreams, and while I'm in them, I cannot understand why other people don't just float themselves up to the sky and join me. It is so easy, nothing to it at all. Most of the time I just spread out my arms and take off, but in one of my dreams I piloted a Frisbee. Now *that* was fun!

But the last dream I had was especially realistic. Once again I was flying, and in my dream I thought to myself, *This is ridiculous. Nobody else is flying except me. I need to find out if this is real or if this is just my imagination.*

So I flew to my parents' home, knocked on the door, and floated up to the ceiling. Then I hovered over my father, who was looking up at me, not at all surprised to find me up there, and I said, "Daddy, listen. You've *got* to tell me the truth. I really think I'm flying. It feels so real. But I'm worried that this might just all be a dream."

My daddy's answer was swift and sure. "Honey," he said, "it's no dream. You're flying all right."

When I woke up I laughed, but then tears welled in my eyes. *How marvelous,* I thought, *that even in my subconscious, in spite of all logic to the contrary, I have a father who believes I can fly.*

For Father's Day last year, I could not find a card that seemed to fit how I felt about Daddy. However, I came across a scene in a children's book that turned out to be perfect. It was a scene with Piglet and Winnie-the-Pooh, walking side by side toward a setting sun. Their short conversation summed up exactly how I felt about my father through the years.

Piglet sidled up to Pooh from behind.

"Pooh!" he whispered.

"Yes, Piglet?"

"Nothing," said Piglet, taking Pooh's paw. "I just wanted to be sure of you."[17]

My dad has been like Pooh to me, his Little Girl-Piglet. Oh, we don't chit-chat a whole lot, not like my mother and I anyway. But in every memory involving my father—from the time he sang, "Put your little foot" as he helped me into my feety pajamas, until this latest dream where he assured me that, yes, I could really fly—my father has been there in the shadows, cheering me on. He has given me the steadfast assurance that always, and forever, I can be sure of him.

And so it is, oh Piglet-Children everywhere, with your Father in heaven.

> *This resurrection life . . . is adventurously*
> *expectant, greeting God with a childlike*
> *"What's next, Papa?"*
> *God's Spirit touches our spirits and confirms*
> *who we really are . . . :*
> *Father and children.*
> *With God on our side like this,*
> *how can we lose?*
> ROMANS 8:14–17, 31, THE MESSAGE

Growing Up to Be a Child

BY BECKY FREEMAN

Mud-puddle miracles
Doodle-bug designs
Bursts of fun with bubblegum
Oh, to see life as a child!

"I love you's" big as rainbows
"I'm sorry's" from the heart
A kiss goodnight, a bear hug tight
To love as would a child!

"Let the children come to Me,"
He said with arms flung wide
Don't stop me now—
I'm coming, too
For I'm a child *inside*

I want to laugh from the belly
Risk playing a clown—
I'm giving up on growing up
Think I'll just start growing

d
o
w
n

Oh, yeeaahh.

"Any of you who welcomes a little child like this
because you are mine,
is welcoming me and caring for me."
MATTHEW 18:5, TLB

Notes

1. Art Linkletter, *The New Kids Say the Darndest Things!* (Ottawa, Ill.: Jameson Books, Inc., 1995), viii.

2. Karol A. Jackowski, *Ten Fun Things to Do before You Die* (Notre Dame, Ind.: Ave Maria Press, 1989), 13–17.

3. Suzanne Lipsett, *Surviving a Writer's Life* (San Francisco: HarperSan Francisco, 1994), 58.

4. L. M. Montgomery, *Anne of Green Gables* (Boston: L. C. Page and Publishers, 1940), 75.

5. Dee Brestin, *The Friendships of Women* (Wheaton, Ill.: Victor Books, 1988), 10.

6. Zick Rubin, *Children's Friendships* (Cambridge, Mass.: Harvard University Press, 1980), 108.

7. Billy and Janice Hughey, compilers, *A Rainbow of Hope* (El Reno, Okla.: Rainbow Studies, Inc.), 198.

8. Paula Hardin, *What Are You Doing with the Rest of Your Life?* (San Rafael, Calif.: New World Library, 1992), 170.

9. Dadi Daley Mackall, *Kids Say the Greatest Things about God* (Wheaton, Ill.: Tyndale House Publishers, 1995), 27.

10. Philip Yancey, *Disappointment with God* (New York: HarperCollins, 1988), 163–64.

11. Colette, "Freedom," *Earthly Paradise*, ed. Robert Phelps (1966), 2; as quoted in Rhoda Thomas Tripp, *International Thesaurus of Quotations* (New York: Harper & Row, 1970), 601.

12. Linkletter, *The New Kids Say the Darndest Things!*, vii.

13. Mackall, *Kids Say the Greatest Things about God*, 73.

14. Ibid., 7.

15. Hardin, *What Are You Doing with the Rest of Your Life?*, 174–75.

16. Ravi Zacharias, *Can Man Live without God?* (Dallas: Word Publishing, 1994), 76.

17. A. A. Milne, *The World of Pooh: The House at Pooh Corner*, "Tigger Unbounced" (New York: Dutton Children's Books, Div. of Penguin USA, 1957; copyright renewed 1985), 261.